36
'Essays
of Engagement'
about
Education

★

Traumear

*

These little essays document my thought during a time when I participated in the daily work of a school and had diverse opportunities for acquainting myself with the concerns and aims of parents, teachers and pupils.

I took an especial interest in the education of our own three children, who became acquainted with both State Education and some home schooling. The youngest, for a few years, attended at a Waldorf School, where I myself participated as a parent. I was able to compare what went on there with State Education and my thinking about education grew to some extent out of that experience.

*

Index

* * *

1. A Comment on Teacher Authority

As soon as a pupil seriously begins to question the authority of the teacher, something in the teacher gives way. That's bound to happen. It's like a kick in the stomach. For four or five years the child looked up to the teacher and mostly accepted whatever came from there, even unquestioningly. Do we expect that the teacher, through those early years, should always have in front of him the moment when the pupil's behaviour becomes - disrespectful? That's how it feels; downright insolent at times. Of course we cannot expect that of him. The teacher gets used to it, to the simple obedience - that isn't actually obedience at all, through those early years, but simple acceptance. Obedience implies that an unwillingness is overcome. Not until now, in the fourth or fifth school year, does the unwillingness lift its head.

The pupil asks, half consciously: "Why do I accept everything so readily? I begin to notice that I have in myself this individual way of looking at things. Am I not being asked here to look at the world through the eyes of my teacher? Let me just see what happens if I insist on my own way."

What an annoyance to the teacher, suddenly! Of course it had never been her intention to force the child's mind into her own way of thinking, but let's face it, until now it just hadn't been an issue. One child's insurrection would be bad enough, but twenty-five! And some of those really make a meal of it. One, if you say black, says white, and vice versa.

The disruption to the normal running of the class seems inexcusable. If only it could be stopped! Usual

1

methods of handling it come to mind. Try the heavy-handed approach, the short, sharp shock - shout at the blighter, a sudden outlet of anger, a bit of violence: you don't really mean it, it's only theatre. But it has the desired effect. Heads go down. A semblance of order is re-established. But only a semblance. Only momentarily. They have only been frightened. And actually, when you think of it, hasn't damage been done? Has unwillingness not been confronted by ill will? And does that not leave a deposit of resentment? Where? In the pupil? Ah, in both; in the teacher too. It's the beginning of behaviour based on fear. The theatre will have to become more realistic. And of course the pupil senses the fear of the teacher; he senses it, if it should come to that, even in the teacher's wrath.

So the teacher scraps that method - of forcing a semblance of discipline. If he loses his temper he doesn't pretend it's his right and privilege to do so, but he apologizes. What a wonderful lesson for the pupil! Here is not fear, but courage. Here, in that apology for a mistake made, he senses in the teacher actual strength. His unwillingness can rise to that, and becomes willingness.

Right, so much for that. The teacher hates to lose his temper, hates it when once again he has frightened a child, but there you go, it happened - he apologizes. It gives him an opportunity to come up with the real goods after all - courage and strength.

Now let's look at the second method; call it the reasonable approach. Be reasonable, says the teacher. I am reasonable with you, now you be reasonable with me. Do I ask of you anything that stresses you, that taxes you, that vexes you? Not at all. You are not being over-worked, I don't lie to you, I give you the benefit of my much more mature experience. And yet there you go again, acting as if I intentionally told you wrong things. Ask questions, by all means, I want you to ask, but why does it every time have to be a challenge? It's almost as if you were obsessed with a desire to show me that every-thing I say can be subverted! Right, so you suppose you are being unfairly treated, unjustly dealt with - we all have to learn to put up with certain unpleasantnesses in our lives. Who said that life was fair? It isn't! Look what I have to put up with from you lot! And do I complain? - Well, yes, as a matter of fact I do. Sorry about that. Back to the drawing-board.

The thing about the reasonable approach is that it doesn't answer to this novel unwillingness of the child, and, more fundamentally, to this growing suspicion in the pupil that there is such a thing in him as the possibility of all liberty from restraint. Call it the hunger for freedom. It will be a while before he learns - if he does eventually learn it - that freedom implies self-imposed work limita-tions. Right now he is simply awakening to this hunger for a liberty from restraint imposed by others, from out-side.

While we sit safe in our living-room, away from the embroilments of the average classroom, we can say: good! It's a good thing that the young human being should discover in himself his own individual will to the future. Of course he has to challenge authority. Do you want him to turn into a slave? into a hypocrite, a sancti-monious purveyor of conventions? Naturally he is bound to mistake those first stirrings of individual liberty for

3

freedom! How can he help himself, he has to test, to experiment, to 'kick against the pricks'. - The teacher walks into the living-room and says: "Alright then, you go into that classroom and try it for yourself. I am fed up to the teeth with it."

So what we are looking for is a fitting response, in the teacher, to the pupil's dawning adulthood - it amounts to that, doesn't it. There is the still vague desire to think and feel for himself. There is the need to act out certain lively and individual impulses even prior to any evident need for them in the outside world. And there is, then, that unwillingness to be told what to do, to be prescribed for, and a growing resentment at being handed the same old recipes for how to be and how to behave. "Be good! Behave yourself!" - On the contrary, says the pupil; to hell with being good. "I want to start being myself - and act!" He is willing to shout it.

How does the teacher, beleaguered by exigencies in the classroom, come up with the suitable response? Certainly at the moment. But so does the angry outburst and the reasonable complaint arise at the moment. The one thing needful is the teacher's authority. Not any delegated authority will do, such as: " - because I am your teacher, and because I am a grown-up with a stick and experience," but authority that arises always and again at the right moment from two things: from quiet reflection on the fact that: "I am by choice the one who comes here precisely in order to respond to this dawning adulthood, no matter how it should turn out that I feel about it," and then from an abiding and repeated intelligent observation, in herself and within herself, of her own individual state of human being, so that she is able to say: Yes, this is anger I feel, and this is impatience, and this is panic. As soon as she honestly identifies these states in herself, how can she help but realize that these are exactly the states of being of the beleaguered pupils - transferred to her! She has here, in herself, the perfect indication of how those pupils at that moment are: they are angry, impatient and in a panic. And she has to have all that in herself if she is even going to begin to respond as an educator.

On the clear recognition and correct interpretation of those states of being depends the teacher's native authority. She cannot explain it, she will refuse to explain it, to justify it, to analyze it. Call it an acquired instinct. It comes about in her while she looks elsewhere. It comes into being and develops organically.

And as soon as she realizes - in the fullest sense of realize - that the states of being she experiences in herself at such moments of crisis are really those of her pupils transferred to her, can she not right away then begin to educate towards adulthood?

If this is how the pupils are right now, she says to herself, then - my heart goes out to them.

She has discovered in herself, once again, the very heart of the pedagogic process. There is definitely compassion, but there is an essential something else, and that is her actual and intense willingness now to suffer those states for her pupils and, by suffering, to end them - thereby creating the space into which the developing pupil can grow.

The educator's compassion is so unique, augmented as it is by - what shall we call it: creative suffering? - that perhaps only our educators know what it amounts to. It is at once a creative way to be and a creative thing to do, and only those who are creative can truly talk about it. That is why we - honour them. We are wise to do so. They occupy a very special position in our midst. Imagine someone who says: I make it my task to deal with your pain so that you can grow.

Of course the teacher's reward is a special one too, and she does not depend on us for it. She does not depend on her pupils' acknowledgment of her authority for her reward. She does not depend for it on our reverence. But we, who have these educators in our midst, do well, for our own sake, to honour them, because that's how we make the best use of their service. While we extend to them our gratitude we are much more likely to benefit from their special skills. And our children, when we send them to these teachers, as pupils, will benefit too from this much more informed attitude towards the educator, as reflected by their parents, who have taken the trouble to learn what real education is about.

So if we narrow our inquiry down again, we might care to consider that a teacher's authority crisis is probably due to the most acute challenge to his profession that he will ever have to face, because his very ability to deal with pain, with guilt and shame, with outrage and indignity is under stress and in question. Every teacher will experience this challenge in his or her own way, because the individual temperament is under strain. It would be immensely valuable if teachers could openly compare how, in the particular, the freedom-pain of their pupils touches on each one of them. That would make for a worthwhile discussion in pedagogics! Because pedagogics has more to do with how a teacher copes in himself than with how he deals outwardly with pupils. But he must recognize the aggravation and frustration he feels as not primarily his own but the pupils', otherwise he cannot appropriately rise to the occasion. No sense just pretending that these feelings are the pupils'. They really are, and they have been transferred to him, and not until he actually knows and believes this can he do for his pupils what he professes to be there to do - to make human growing-space for them.

The teacher's native authority will come out clear and strong, and the pupils will say: "Yes, this is what it was all about," as soon as the teacher shows by his example that these growing-pains attached to every experience of freedom are finally nothing to worry about because they can be handled. The pupil will become like putty in his hands as soon as the teacher manifests this authority.

And this is by no means an ideal, but a way of more or less doing something. "Suffer the children to come unto me," said the educator of us all who lives in our hearts and shows us how to suffer right now by his own example. As soon as we have trouble with this transferred pain, why not transfer it to him? He is willing and more than glad to educate right here and now beside us in the classroom.

We cannot deal with this pain while we assume that it originates in ourselves. We can repress it, become callous to it, become embittered and resentful in reaction to it, and finally we either burn out or break down. We cannot blame our pupils. They only demand from the teacher what the teacher is offering by being there: the authority to deal with the pain in connection with growing up and in relation to an education towards a workable freedom.

This authority crisis occurs at such a crucial time in a child's life because here he comes up for the first time against the opportunity to behave morally and ethically - and naturally it frightens him. He has never responded to such a desire in his nature before. We might call it the virtual drive. Since he cannot right away just deal with it, he feels impotent, put upon, unjustly treated. Naturally he is more than glad to be able to pass on such feelings to an adult near him who is accomplished.

And the very root of all virtue is that certain love through which we manage to suffer one another's pain. The teacher who does that for a pupil plants a seed that will eventually sprout as human virtue. So on the occasion of this authority crisis, the educator has the golden opportunity for sowing, in the pupil, that unique seed which will later on grow as the ability to do good and as the willingness to behave lovingly towards others, even towards those he dislikes. Such an ability is after all exactly what the teacher exercises when she responds to an authority crisis in herself by gladly suffering the moral and ethical growing-pains of her pupils as transferred to herself.

* * *

2. Anxiety

There must be a way of dealing with anxiety. Or, let me put it this way: there must be something I can do right now, when I'm not anxious, to make it more likely that I'll be able to deal with anxiety next time I'm anxious. I'm not trying to prevent myself from becoming anxious;

8

I've given up on that. It's a tremendous breakthrough, for me, to be able to admit to myself that I will very likely feel anxious, and even be anxious, again, soon. This doesn't mean that I've given up in any way; on the contrary. It means that I'm convinced that somehow, in some light yet to be discovered, anxiety in itself is no big deal; it all depends on what I make of it. In fact it depends on whether I make something of it or lie down under it - whether I'm intelligently capable in the face of it or else resist it and get fearfully snared up in it.

It's silly to say: Don't be afraid of anxiety, it can't hurt you. It's not wrong, it's just a silly thing to say, because anxiety is in itself a fear that fear can hurt us. It seems equally useless to try to solve this problem of anxiety by attempting to come to terms, rationally and reasonably, with what we assume, upon detailed analysis, might be the cause for some particular anxiety. Momentary relief might be the outcome of that, which is often a great help, but at the moment I'm on the look-out for something more permanent.

The opposite of fear is courage. Now if anxiety is the fear of fear, than the opposite of anxiety must be something like the courage for courage. Does that make any sense? More to the point, will that make sense to me the next time I'm anxious?

I'm willing to try it. In order to be able to give it a fair go when the time comes, I ought to elaborate here and now on what I mean by 'the courage for courage'. It came to me as a genuine thought, so I intend to respect it, to give it the benefit of the doubt.

9

Courage is unique. How? It's based on power and it's powerful. When I am courageous, I rely on a certain power and I am powerful. A quick definition of power: the good in action. Those who are powerful can stand up in the face of evil; they remain undaunted, unhindered, by evil. (I want to get to the heart of the matter because I've allowed myself only five pages.) Is this power accessible for me? Can I be powerful? I don't have to look very far - I'm drawing on that power right now. So are you, if you're trying to follow my reasoning. This power is closer to us than our own self. That's saying a lot. This power stands between me and my self. So, enigmatically, I have to let go of my self in order to contact this power. Better yet, as soon as I intentionally let go of my self - I'm powerful.

An interesting development. The emphasis now is on how to let go of my self. First of all I would have to admit that I am attached to my self, that I in fact hug such a thing as my self to myself and that this self is customarily my immediate and automatic resource when I'm in any kind of trouble at all. I would even go so far as to maintain that any kind of trouble at all is essentially my attachment to my self as a resource. Some resource! On experience, I cannot recommend it. I'm convinced my self is unreliable, disrespectful, foolish and cowardly. What's yours? It's bound to be different.

I must admit I feel better after that confession. I'm not talking about me, by the way, but about my self. I mention this in case you think I'm putting myself down. What I am putting down is the cowardice, foolishness, disrespectfulness and unreliability to which I in particular am prone. I renounce them.

But back they come as soon as my supremacy is challenged. Good intentions are not enough. I will have to work on this for the next fifty years. I will have to make a habit of ridding myself of my self. The first time I did it I was powerful for a moment, and that moment stayed with me. I know now how to achieve that power and how to pile it up. I can do that, for example, by sharing it with you, as I do right now. It increases as I exercise it for others. Equally it decreases while I hug it to myself. A lot depends now on how persistently I can keep up this activity of power sharing. I shall try to make more of your welfare than of my own. When I look across to you, to who you are, how you are and what you are, taking an interest for the purpose of somehow becoming one with you, one in soul and spirit, I see something that opens my eyes even wider. I see the strength that underpins the world.

Rather amazing, this. The same strength I experience in myself experiences itself out there. I can step out there and be among friends. I give myself a bit of a jolt and step out. There, that took courage. I like the fresh air and the sunshine. Alright, so it's the middle of the night in my room, but take my word for it, I enjoy the fresh air and the sunshine all the same. Suddenly there is no more 'out there'. I'm out here now. In a very important sense I've arrived.

What happens now is a bit of a blow to me. I imagined I might be able to rest on my laurels. Instead I'm under siege and under attack. Really, I am. Forces and energies pile in on me. They contest my happiness. They sour my satisfaction. They embitter me and make me resentful.

Very well, I had courage once, and I can have it again. "Why do they bother with me, these forces and energies?" I ask myself. Evidently they want what I have. Their disturbing existence in my life shall mean to me nothing more than that I possess something worthwhile. Negative and positive forces, exhausting and exciting energies - I am going to have to keep them in perspective. If they lull me, I lose track. If they liberate me, I become careless. I don't want to be liberated or lulled by these energies and forces that didn't show up until I had power out here, power for you and me. You and I are human beings. These forces and energies are not. I sincerely believe they are jealous of our powerful humanity. Does that make sense?

The question is: Are they of any use to me? Because anxiety, when it arises, forces me to suspect that I have not arrived powerfully after all. I fear that the strength I have experienced in the world and myself was after all but illusion, and that the courage that took me out here was misguided. Anxiety is the fear that we are going to slide back into our previous unconsciousness. That is evidently where these forces and energies would prefer us.

Not our arrival is illusion, but these powers and energies are - delusion. Anxiety would alert us to that. And our powerful task, after having arrived, consciously, out here, is to overcome these delusive energies and forces so as to become more than conscious, namely aware.

Anxiety is to alert me to a danger of delusion. Consequently it can also be taken as the signal for an opportunity. The time is ripe for greater awareness. A force, an energy, can be overcome. Identify it and know it as delusion. We know these forces and energies to be overcome by the way they affect our best interests and plans. Something we ourselves have projected into the future is frustrated. The light we depended on to steer our course wisely through the world grows dim. A perfectly sober rationale from yesterday holds no water today. If nothing comes along to shake us out of our stupor we resign ourselves to apathy. At a moment's notice we dash off to exert ourselves because doing so makes us feel better. - All these are points of delusion to be overcome. We can take our time with them. The anxiety has long ago passed but we keep pushing forward, gently and sensitively, and above all courageously. This is courage beyond courage. We began with the courage to face and interpret our anxiety. We went on with the courage to overcome delusion upon delusion.

Naturally others gain something now from the way we behave. There is a product, a work. Gradually awareness grows in us, we can barely say how. Where consciousness drew us and provoked us, awareness now shines all around us and through us. We can see once again the strength in the world and in us, but now this strength is a principle of growth, a pattern of our behaviour, the meaning of our being. We ourselves have become strong.

We can go now from strength to strength, because we know how to take advantage of our anxieties. If we had no power we could not become anxious. Since we have power we may exercise it courageously. When those energies and forces, those false powers, besiege or attack us, we no longer need to be alerted by anxiety, because we know how to right away overcome, by courting awareness and by knowing delusions as delusions rather than paling before them or entering into futile contest with them.

Consciousness alone is not enough, we are forced to come to terms with that nowadays. The desire to remain conscious must be replaced by the will to become aware. Our human strength demands to be acknowledged, in awareness. Anxiety makes good sense as a pointer in that worthwhile direction.

* * *

3. Communion

We can barely begin to suggest where our own zone of personal influence ends and that of another begins. Usually when we feel lost in ourselves and the other one only disturbs our misery, the slightest depression fuels the flames of a self-consuming, impervious anger. Why are we angry? Or why are we morbid? Our link with our fellow communicant no longer exists. Those most commonly on the same wave-length with us have switched to another, more intimate channel, and it excludes us.

Therefore we make ourselves pleasant, and often we lie, to avoid the shame of a lonely existence. Nevertheless it behoves us to cancel these faulty connections from time to time, and then our society ails or is strained. We have limited means for consulting our heart, which is not always trustworthy in any case. Why should it matter that we mend the rupture between person and person? Why have we so much to lose, if we leave ourselves transient?

The man who scolds his environment because he does not fit into it is a menace to those who have learned how to win and behave. Evidence lets us conclude our complaint if we patiently wait for it. The salto mortale out of basic existence into meaningful life is managed by those who rectify less than they dare.

The inward journey is fraught with rage and indifference. A simple kindliness sometimes does more to propel the creative engine forward than a heap of discussion or reams of analysis. And next to kindliness stands, with his face somewhat averted, the angel of mercy. We are awkward in his presence. Out of his eyes, if our destiny, bids him glance for a moment in our direction, terror inspirits us, horror penetrates our indigent soul. This is impossible! Mercy is surely a welcome experience! There are those who swear that if mercy reigned, all would prosper.

A matter of opinion? Man is to man a retreat from truth or a bold overcoming. What we contain in our hearts prevents us from facing the issue of heightened experience. Influence nags us to death, it seems. Our exaggerated senses are barely accessible to love from within. Where it urges, we are drawn from our stilted purpose and our harvest is hatred. So few have succeeded with inward impressions, with the easy silence that is eloquence personified, with the cool assortment of language particulars sprung from chaos complying with a smile, that communion seems less than a byword. Who knows communion? Who can ingest the difference between self and ego and hold his tongue, not boast his achievement?

Why has communion slipped down into cracks in the earth's surface and each of us stands in perverse isolation? Am I polite? You spit on my politeness. Our social contract is to murder truth, not boldly uphold it. In a

15

sickening sphere of timid delusion we breathe one another's cruel exhalations. Ours is a tragic lot, modern and merciless. By the banks of the stream of life we are bound by an oath to turn thirst into virtue, to reward with prestige restraint from bathing. It appears that if ever we are to succeed we must fail first and suffer frustration. Anodyne pleasure remains miraculous, a mirage of hope, an ideal construction held at arm's length beyond death and the grave, while narcotic pleasures are plucked from the flesh in premature haste, while evil grins.

Communion works if you learn who yourself is and then make allowances for those who have nothing. Communion works if you know who yourself is and then take care to share that knowledge. Trust the one next to you with your integral attention. We have paid such attention to things that belonged to us and to people whose presence and company we valued, but did we do it in the knowledge of what we were doing and in the recognition of what was being achieved? For here is a remarkable thing, which on the surface seems anything but remarkable, that it makes a fundamental difference to what we are doing if we know what we do. And if in addition we are mindful of the achievement though we have no sign of it, then we are effective to the point not only of competence, but beyond, to excellence. And to excel in matters of personal communication is a goal worthy of pursuit. There are those who suppose they can do it without being changed in the process, and they are wrong. There are those who fear to do it because they suspect they must be changed in the process, and they are right. They are right even to fear, but not wise to let that fear prevent them, for in that fear, if they lower themselves into it or else rise into it, whichever seems most appropriate at the time, they are purged of what stands between them and their change.

Never mind even guessing the profile of the change. Call it maturity, call it growth, evolution. Know only that we are all being changed; unless we fear, being modern, and then we will be changed; unless we offer obstruction, of arrogance or cowardice, and then we must be changed, which is a downright nuisance, because all we ever experience of our glorious metamorphosis is the dissolution of the previous stage, the disintegration of the previous case. The modern man at least looks forward to what he might have right now if he bothered to get his act together, if he threw away his ritual symbols and allegories and reached for the concrete, and so he has something like a foretaste of what contemporary men, women and children have as their life right now. But the poor man who shuns every move to improve him is deprived even of his ability to resist, and then there's and end to that.

Once we have come into the way of communion we can clearly distinguish these three: hell, earth without heaven and heaven on earth, and it makes us glad that even that is a good way of putting it.

So when we meet to spend time in fellowship we may aim for communion and know that we are both being changed. It may not feel good, but then we move into that, glad to be purged.

When two or three meet, communion is possible. But keep this as a secret. As soon as you build up a monument to set it off and as soon as you point to yourself and say: Here I am doing it - it leaves and moves elsewhere.

What is it? The one. Who is it? The one. You can make yourself out to be servant of servants or lord of lords but nothing works out if the one does not find you. Where will it find you? In communion with two or three. What can you do, to be where he cannot but find you? Learn of communion. First learn to hear and to see. Then take an interest. Learn to distinguish the being within you from outward concerns. Then make your choice. Others are here to invite you to share. Do it more willingly. Give of your riches; be generous and prudent. Observe how your talk. Your speech and language, either helps or hinders. Wonder about that. Might you be more effective?

Shun all magic. Avoid charisma. You were born with a brain, use it impartially. Oh, that the best part of man-kindly strength should be lost in confusion! You were born with a brain, but you waste it on trivia. The poor person next to you leads an existence that resembles yours in substance and detail, and yet you behave as if trauma drew down on you strict isolation in terms of your spirit and soul. Pain is to make us more communicable. Injury is to prevent us from prospering out of bounds where life and humanity are at odds. Communion sanctions the one I am in favour of the one you are.

* * *

4. Community and Democracy

How we get on with others, how we manage in their presence and what benefit we draw from their company, these are common areas of concern here.

Democracy is an invention, an expedient. People can manage more easily if they know ahead of time how far they can go before risks are taken, before individual plans trespass on another man's territory. Legislation can be enforced democratically.

Community is a concept that legislates in its own right. A communal decision happens as much as it is taken. The members of a community cannot be externally defined; each one knows himself to be a communal being, at a certain time, and acts accordingly, quite irrespective of such a thing as a collective entity.

Democracy has meaning only with respect to a collective entity, externally identifiable. A certain group of people collates opinions, canvasses desires, recognizes needs - as a group, as a number of individuals who agree for the time being on belonging to this group. Each individual contracts into the ethos of the group by paying with individual rights for personal liberties. A democratic decision allows me to graze my sheep on the common, and one has arrived at that decision democratically by assuring that no other member of the group is disadvantaged by what I propose to do. So the element of independence is crucial. In terms of democracy one seeks out neutral areas of interest and makes them available for use.

Where community has taken hold, democracy is no longer necessary, because individuals have enjoyed a taste of personal freedom. These persons, now, are able to behave productively and, for example, to make their wishes known without right away demanding satisfaction. The community of which they are members guarantees their mutual dependence. A member of a community works to depend on other members. He feels enlarged and refined by this dependence because it opens him up inwardly to a higher, more lively plane of reality where he can be himself more truly. A democratic process would interfere with this because it would emphasize as worthwhile something that makes no sense within the communal framework, namely the rights of the individual. Such rights have become irrelevant, not unimportant, to the communal person. He still respects those rights wherever no communality exists, but for himself and for the other members of his community individual rights, or the rights of individuals, cannot come into the equation. They do not signify. As soon as they do, he is no longer a communal being.

Democracy pertains to society. The social sacrifice is made so that social values are protected. Within society there are those who hope to gain from their dependence upon, and connection with, the fabric of it, and they respect one another for those claims upon values based on likeness. Every democratic process operates in terms of such a likely issue, or in terms of several of them. Prior to the commencement of the process, links must exist between people based on common tendencies and habits of choice.

Community, by comparison, cuts across all such areas of similar inclination and operates from basic human faculties, such as imagination, love, understanding, etc. Society does not operate from such as these and therefore it reveals perpetually a bias which must be corrected, such as by way of the democratic process. Such corrections, if it were but known, point social individuals in the direction of community, and every now and again a personal spark leaps, society is left behind and the 'result', if one may put it that way, is a communal human being, no longer socially definable.

Eventually we quite human-naturally desire to move away from society and towards a community. But once we have tasted the communal predilection we have no quarrel with society or with its means and measures, because the influence we hope to exercise springs from our human natural faculties, to which we may directly apply, and not from rights of individuality, which must perpetually be fought for and protected, perhaps democratically. Democracy as a system of political endeavour, for example, presupposes a degree of unconsciousness, in the face of thought, feeling and will for example, sufficient to allow accidental stirrings of these to move to the forefront and claim priority attention. Not human faculties, but popular notions become current and - require repeated correction, ostensibly in the direction of individual liberties but in fact so that a degree of reasonable consciousness might be achieved.

*

A declared interest in the democratic process type-casts people as 'on the way to liberty and freedom'. From within a social awareness, however, true freedom is in no way fathomable, but only glimpsed as through a screen. Society deals in parables, and democracy is an exercise in metaphor, but metaphors are taken for truths by the members of society. Any attempt therefore to make democracy do duty directly to communal ends can only be counterproductive; the implication here is that members of a community would forgive the democratic infringement and utilize the opportunity in the interest of increased communality. (One of the divinity's many mysterious ways.)

This raises the issue of communal confidence and strength. How far can anyone be said to be along the way towards a true communal awareness? No external measurement, such as social standing, prestige, etc. as in the case of society, is available. Those who would like to be socially committed, socially above suspicion and such like, have a ready index for their ambition in the eyes of others. How do the members of a community track their record? They dare not manipulate one another's regard. Since the communal move is towards personal dependence, not independent individuality, there must be something that actually counteracts any tendency, or liability, to the democratically correctable social sphere. No one is mechanically locked into personhood.

This something has to do with our commitment to our functioning human faculties, to such spontaneous motivations as conscience, intelligence and good will. The name we would give it is self-examination. One might say that self-examination does for community what democracy does for society, keeping in mind that communal aims cannot be compared, and share no common denominator with, social goals. A social being would think of self-examination in terms of self-analysis, whereby hindrances to sociability are removed, as witness an extreme example of this in the case of communist socialism, in the public realm, or in the private sphere as advocated initially by S. Freud and subsequently by practitioners of psychiatry.

In the communal spirit, however, self-examination does not impinge upon public policy or private points of view, but a person checks on his rootedness in humanity and reviews his commitment to human being. We can sense how democracy is a shadow of this on the other side of the divide. My rigorous examination of my self dissolves it, so that once again I may share in community with you. As a member of society I would have examined my self so that it might shine spotless under the gaze of the world or so that I myself might be persuaded of its justifiable rightness (righteousness). A member of society, or a social being, is fearful of incrimination, by himself or his fellow man, and he 'creates' societies (religions, sects, political parties, clubs) so as to pool his resources of justification, and always of course in comparison to, in competition with, and in a degree of animosity against other and lesser societies.

A communal being is less worried about being accused and found out than about being selfish. He examines himself so as to be less liable to selfishness, for he understands, and has learned from repeated painful experience, that through selfishness he muddies the communal spring and severs the communal link of fruitful personal dependence.

But selfishness prevails where the self is not removed, just as in the case of society some such corrective as democracy is required if the rights of the individual are not to be trodden underfoot.

The integrity of individuals is, of course, not ignore where the communal spirit is embodied and wrought forth as ethical action and behaviour. It is not ignored, but not specifically attended to either. We always and again make the mistake of supposing that a community is similar to a society, or a kind of society. The communal spirit "moves as it listeth", and we might as readily balance water on a pin as wrest from this spirit a workable prediction. We can act in its name all the time however, and be ready for its visitation, just so that we know it from other spirits and understand its unique challenges and singular rewards. Those who call themselves members of a particular externally identifiably community invite precisely an uncertainty with respect to their action and behaviour, because the communal spirit will not be limited by appearances, and by the sort of thing that allows us to schedule and label.

What may happen then is that such a lapsed community, having lapsed into moral stagnation or into spiritual arrogance, refuses to examine itself, each person individually on his own volition, and so persists in a collective selfishness, morbidly inturned or absurdly out for world conquest. It even assumes the trappings of a society, even calls itself a society, and then presents itself to the informed eye as a most strange phenomenon indeed, like a tree that tries to sprout wings, or like a horse that wants to take root. For example, democratic decisions are taken so as to boost the collective morale, or an enchantment with democratic process lifts everyday concerns into the realm of the charismatic. When that happens one feels inclined to step back and wash one's hands of the entire affair.

But a single human being with a head on his shoulders and a heart in his breast can work wonders, literally. It suffices to be around, to stay put and to be still. Suddenly the communal spirit once again finds a handhold and a foothold, and matters that were dead begin to move while spectral phenomena simply pass out of countenance. One true person suffices to afford this spirit once again entry where laziness and badness had blocked its path.

But it must be a person and not an individual. A person by definition communes. What does it mean to commune? It means to lay aside every vestige of conceit and self-centricity while probing and exercising the faculty of creative inwardness. Such communion makes for the healing and health of every community. It should not be confused with communication. Communion is done by one, for the benefit of a few, of several and of many. It can turn the course of history and change the face of the earth. And no one else really needs to know that it goes on. We can take it for granted that where communion is done the communal spirit takes hold. Then we may observe the effects of purification and cleansing. Where there was disorder, we observe discipline and peace. The usual business of the day is managed, but no longer under stress and in turmoil.

No one in his right mind desires, and certainly no one deserves, credit for the communal spirit. Communion is its own reward, and in that respect it compares to self-examination for dissolution of self. The parallel in society is the once and for all time democratically elected benevolent dictator, the worldly messiah.

* * *

5. Contemporary Wisdom

The question we wish to ask here is: Can wisdom be contemporary? Some things disappear when they are hauled into the light of day, and this has to do with the nature of the light of day, which banishes spectres, phantoms and all spirits that are not good. In the light of day, which is contemporary, only good spirit can prevail. This is because the light of day is itself one of the many manifestations of the spirit that is good.

Statements such as these are not calculated to win friends and influence people. There is a way of discussing matters that pertain to knowledge and understanding that derives from time-honoured methods, and sometimes such a thing as a science is advanced a bit by a new slant on the way experience is thought and talked about. There has, however, always been a wisdom that has never advanced and never will advance, simply because it is not that sort of wisdom. It makes good sense to simply call it wisdom, and to refrain entirely from calling it one kind of wisdom or another. As old as man is the nature of this wisdom, and if man can be said to be old, then the same goes for this wisdom.

But the nature of this wisdom dictates that man is not old, and that neither is he young because man is a concept, a myth, or an idea, but not a reality. The fact that man is not real has to be accepted if we are to appreciate that men, women and children are real. In comparison to men, women and children, man is a way of conducting our imagination into the realm of fantasy and dream.

But precisely these two, fantasy and dream, exist to serve reality, and it is in the service of real down to earth existences that they find their sole justification. Outside this realm they lose themselves as spectres and phantoms. All such tricks of the imagination should be avoided as soon as they are identified, and then our imagination should once again be pressed into the service of contemporary reality, which comprises all things and persons that participate in good spirit and embody it.

*

If we allow that such a thing as wisdom pure and simple has always existed, then it remains to be asked: Have human beings always been equally capable of being wise? The notion of wisdom as something that can be accessed by those who would be wise is not all that far-fetched. What rarely happens is that anyone dedicates his working life to the acquisition of wisdom and realizes at the same time that the wisdom he means is given at birth to children.

Like a luminous sphere above mankind hangs the goal of their dreams. Who are they, the representatives of the human race who take upon themselves every now and again a renewal of what has been and of what will be? Do we say they are sent? And do we necessarily like what they bring? That someone should say there is one god alone who has all things in hand is certainly astonishing, considering his cultural environment at the time. But that someone else should turn up shortly after and feel himself singled out as human representative of that god is not so much astonishing as to be expected.

We have suddenly moved from the realm of the speculative intellect into the sphere of that wisdom as previously announced by that intellect. Such a move was intended to illustrate something of the impact, on our human mind, of eternal wisdom as alive in babes and as perceptible and practicable at once by some mature adults. Our concept of human maturity fits very nicely, as it happens, with the work of this wisdom. If the effect of this work is sometimes that our intellectual breath is taken away, this should not surprise us. Wisdom counsels from our heart while our head is alert, whereas all matters intellectual at best approach the heart.

If our head were not alert, the heart would take matters into its own hands and stray from the path of integrity. Those who are seriously dedicated to the pursuit of wisdom are aware of this risk and they learn their craft with that in mind. The work of true wisdom embraces the entire human being and is therefore of no use to those who insist on a partial reference. To them there is nothing to be said except: "Do as you may. You are persuaded of your perfect propriety and you do have the collective on your side, what more could you want?"

If we tentatively leave ourselves in the hands of this wisdom we are informed of many things. First we ourselves are informed, for our own purpose chiefly, while we attain to a certain degree of inward development. Then we are supplied with information for others. The canonical essence of this information sets it apart, we should never suppose that it can be otherwise. Our intelligence would not stand for it if we allowed ourselves any leeway at all in the interpretation of what is an intimate revelation, for the hearts and minds of those who have hearts and minds. Of course we will stray momentarily from the path but one of our functions is precisely the repeated rediscovery of the central wisdom from among a great variety of directions, whence we return, having imbibed the afflictions and agonies of others.

Even in this present piece of work we have an excellent example of how the nausea of insignificance is overcome in the interest of a far-sighted purpose which cannot be defined until after it is attained.

*

Contemporary wisdom derives equally from the divinity of man and from the humanity of god. Our wishful thinking is out of the question inasmuch as we see precisely what we do as we do it, and this in itself is not patient of imitation. No longer do we order our lives in one sense and live it in another, so that neither the plan nor the realization of it match our soul or spirit, so that consequently we have neither joy nor contentment. This wisdom, by comparison, begins where the old heaven and the old earth have disappeared and it advocates world without end. We engage the spirits that mean us well and revoke those whose origin is not ours. We are joined in the past and are one in the future, while all life takes place here and now eternally. Time endlessly plays into our hands. Whoever has access to this wisdom makes no bones about it but fits himself into the infinite scheme of things for the purpose of final achievements.

How does this wisdom vary from person to person? As one person differs from the other. No room here for dalliance with strange men's fancies, since each must speak with his own voice, give shape to things with his own hand, and no time for contentiousness. And he who remains aloof from the joys and sorrows of his fellow men, women and children has no such wisdom for his source but a pallid resemblance of it, which may cause him to hide behind the fog of his own jargon.

He who has not in his nature the personal truth has no right to speak of contemporary wisdom. He who is bloated

29

with enthusiasm because nothing substantially takes hold in him causes others to go blind.

How can anyone call himself wise? There is nothing to be gained by doing so. We are wise when we know how ignorant we are and ignorant when we deem ourselves wise. Or should wisdom be pursued like a career? Are there experts in the manner of wisdom?

This divine/human wisdom is not to be scheduled or abbreviated. The man who supposes himself to have a right to it soon finds himself disowned by it, and thereafter his words are chaff. No one has invented it and no one has discovered it. But those who speak from a pure heart and a clear head find this wisdom even on their lips, and the taste of it is sweet.

Avail yourself of it as though it were the most precious commodity. Rather than discussing it in public know it in secret. Press yourself against it as to a beloved one and know it as flesh of your flesh, spirit of your spirit. The annoyance is always that others refuse to acknowledge your superiority. Not you are superior, but your wisdom. Let it be your wisdom then and draw no attention to yourself, so that your works may speak for you.

Know that this wisdom of man and of god in one is productive of good works and you will not be able to help it. The very joy of creativity will break out of you like jubilation. What, have you no strength? No vitality? no certainty in your life? You are suspicious, fearful, quick to find fault? Then this wisdom has no room in you but you do in your misery have what it takes to make that room. In your cowardice your courage is wisely rendered. In your weakness wisdom puts down roots of strength.

Your self-doubt wisely begets certainty. Works such as these are always and again the beginning and they must come before the works that give courage, strength and certainty to others. As soon as you are healed, you radiate health effectively. No need to speak; it suffices to be.

*

Poor men lift themselves up and beyond the lot of their neighbour so as not to be affected, but the wisdom we mean here dictates another course. Seek out the condition of those who are near you and make yourself at home there. Lead such a life that the anger welling up in you in the face of wide-spread ignorance is right away transmuted into helpful education. Entertain only such systems of belief as visibly comfort those, at the moment, who would otherwise be destitute, spiritually, or deprived, naturally. Let the length and breadth of your interest and ambition mesh in with the cares and concerns of human beings and leave people to look after themselves, as they will do in any case.

This wisdom, by definition, cannot be other than contemporary. However, those who associate in the name of it are liable to risk misconstruance and to forfeit effectiveness, as witness, once again, the abyss that opens, symptomatically, between past satisfactions and future consolations. Where individual responsibility is not cheerfully grasped, such a judgment must enter, so that once again the reality, which in truth is here and now, must appear, in modern fashion, faded and at best aspirational.

So when we speak of 'contemporary' wisdom, specifically, we do so in the hope of effecting a correction, - not in the wisdom that is as it remains, but in our attitude, that is liable to all the usual aberration due to uninvested enthusiasm and short-sightedness. An insistence on the contemporary roots and fruits of this wisdom forces us to get our brains into gear, so that we learn to trust the necessary inspiration of every local moment. The demands that are made on the globe today, universally, are equally made on each one of us, in terms of each detail of our daily existence. My own personal conscience, not allegories of myths and mystiques, constitutes the key to any lasting good that can be done by me. An ethic of chastity, fidelity and moral creativity prepares me for wisdom, and this ethic must be lived, through the daily grind of achievement and error. Then I can finally say: Now I espouse contemporary wisdom. Now I partake of the wisdom that affords real insight and empowers with genuine humanity.

Wisdom is contemporary in that it combines action and passion right now with the immediate reward of knowing that what we do is not wasted and cannot fail. We do good if we do it for one another, chiefly and initially within ourselves, where people cannot tell but our god co-operates.

* * *

6. Creative Education

We think of education as first and foremost the province of teachers. Teachers, we suppose, feel a sort of divine calling to teach, they are born with a talent for getting on with groups of children in classrooms and they have been adequately trained to impart knowledge of the right sort at the proper time for a good reason. We, as parents, trust them to treat our children in the classroom as we would have them treated. We would like them to set good examples as human beings and beyond that there is the curriculum. We have insight into the curriculum and although we cannot be expected to set it, we reserve the right to comment.

The state school system is a cumbrous affair. We look around, to see if we can do better for our offspring. We come across a creative school. Here we seem to have education based less on the need to raise the GNP and more on a vision of the child. We have an approach to education that has as its priority something like the organic development of children. Intellectuality takes second place and in the forefront there is an appeal to the whole child.

How creative education compares to state education - to any state education - is a study in itself. One might look at the difference in nature, in addition to any difference in quality. Then, we can talk about creative education in theory, on one side, and on the other side we can look at the practice, at any particular school. We might, for example, like what goes on at a particular creative school precisely because that school has improved on the approach introduced by the founder, if there is one. Variation from the orthodox does not necessarily imply less quality.

Where the existence of a school originates, at least to some extent, in specific preferences of a community, something unique is going on. Here parents have certain identifiable aspirations for their children that cannot be met, or that can only to a lesser degree be met, by nearby state schools or, for that matter, by any state school. The responsibility parents choose to take upon themselves in this case is worth looking at. It does not begin with the business of getting the child to set off to school on time and it does not end with help with the homework. It begins with the choice of a particular stimulus in the child's life and ends, or rather continues, with a constant and repeated discernment of that stimulus.

Let's call it the creative educational stimulus and let's admit at the outset how it must be a communal one. No single person can be made responsible for it. Life itself is not possible in the end except as an ethical entity, and similarly for this enlivening stimulus: it must originate from a few, from several or from many, who specifically get together for the purpose of defining, describing and directing it. What a single person can do is point out that this is so and call for a concerted effort. The stimulus does not come first, and then more and more people are swept away by it. Such an impulse is not creative but influences us at football games, at concert halls and at evangelist rallies and is at best recreational.

So the need can be identified by one person, the nature of the satisfaction can be described by another, who has experienced it, but several persons must get together for a meeting of hearts and minds before this creative stimulus can actually become flesh.

This being the nature of creative education, we should not expect it to flourish unless attention is paid, in the right sort of awareness. By the right sort of awareness I mean perfect good will at the exclusion of any and all criticism. Creativity cannot respond to coercion or seduction. In that way one can force a standard or keep up appearances, no more. Creative education, however, is not a standard and cannot be compared to a standard.

*

A special school that aims at creative education needs at least a few persons who make the creative educational stimulus their business. At least a few, perhaps several, must put themselves at the service of the very heartbeat of the school. They are the ones who understand and believe that the spirit of the school must come before any- and everything else. No amount of money can pay for this spirit. Sufficient money will, however, become available while the spirit of the school lives. A school rich in money is not necessarily a creative school; the presence or absence of money signifies nothing on that score. What we can take for granted is that a financial impulse is worthless. Money as an attempt to improve the quality of a creative school is a nonstarter.

How can a few make a difference to the spirit, to the creative impulse of a school?

They are the ones who understand best how this spirit moves. They know of the source of all good spirit. They are themselves familiar with some of the aspects of human creativity, especially with its communal dimension. They delight in human relationship and in its knock-on effect. And above all they share an insight into the necessary spontaneity of all action that is truly good.

First we must be, then we can do. Availability to creative spontaneity is a crucial way of being. Thereafter, at each point in time, arrive notions as to what might be undertaken or done. It can never be a case of: Let's try this or that, to see if it works. Whatever is done in this communal spirit of creativity works, though one can never say ahead of time what particular good effect it will have. The very existence of those who together have the creative spirit of a school at heart works and has a good effect.

Why bother? So that a few children at least might appreciate their childhood and look forward to growing up. And who knows how many grown-ups can be helped to re-discover their childhood!

*

The difference between standard and creative education is like that between night and day. We should never tire of persuading ourselves of that difference, of keeping our eyes open to it.

The danger is, that those who foster creative education and are in favour of it suppose they can do away with standards. They have experienced how work to a standard makes for competition and coercion. Perhaps they have suffered under the pressure of authoritarianism that is usually implied by such work. They have not been able to turn themselves into mindless slaves, but neither have they managed to push through to personal freedom, in which the standard cross is born. The advent of creative education, for them, means mostly a lack of pressure and the absence of hard labour and of force from outside. While their attitude is understandable and their disposition forgivable, they are all the same unformed and misguided. Creative education is not standard education minus the hardships. Creative education is not achieved when we do away with standards and substitute wishful thinking and fond hope. All the same, creative education is not education to a standard.

*

This comparison of 'standard' and 'creative' has, of course, application outside and beyond the topic of education. We cannot, however, discuss any creative education unless we make reference to that comparison.

One tends to forget, perhaps, why standards were invented in the first place. We can see them as attempts to forestall an imagined catastrophe. We can understand them as expedients, set up to deal with experienced setbacks and bad tendencies. Standards are relatively modern inventions, halfway between law and freedom from the law. They stem from the often quite serious desire to render relatively permanent and to extend, as an insurance into the future, a certain forward momentum in terms of quality and value. As anyone knows who has read or travelled a bit, standards vary from location to location, from people to people and from time to time. We come across standards of forceful activity, of contemplative leisure, of reward-orientation, of dwelling-in-the-process. Moral standards can be worldly, pious, philosophical, Calvinist and so on, endlessly. What they all have in common is that more or less well informed ambition to safeguard a possession and to progress in some virtue.

The bitter pill we all have to swallow eventually in reference to standards is that they cannot last. They break down under their own cumbersome insistence on observance or they lift off the ground and float off into the stratosphere of ineffectual or fanatical idealism. That is why new standards are invented to replace the old. For a time these replacements are mistaken for the final solution, then disappointment sets in again and disenchantment surfaces.

Eventually, especially in the lives of certain individuals, this temporal nature of standards in general is experienced as a horror and as a shame. The reason for such an experience is not tiredness, laziness or moral fatigue, but an insight into something like creative reality, where one actually takes hold of something that lasts. When the works of such creative persons become public property they are also frequently misunderstood. Where the law was in fact completed it is supposed to have been dismissed. Turmoil sets in. To deal with the chaos, systems of standards are set up, break down, are replaced, and the typically modern pendulum continues to swing, between rationality and irrationality, between stoic self-constraint and lavish renaissance enlightenment, between insistence on order and liberty from crippling constraint. We have nearly had two thousand years of it.

There have always been a few who did not mistake the consummation of the law for its dismissal, but due to overwhelming competition from the standard fashion of the day they have chosen to remain relatively anonymous, or at least they have kept out of the fray of competition for prestige and prizes.

Steiner education, at a Waldorf School, for example is purportedly a type of creative education where standards of behaviour, of thinking, even of being, are therefore not goals. But neither are they dropped. Those who enter upon such a course of education out of defeatism, or out of a sense of disillusion over standard education, and not much else, are literally worse off than if they had maintained a standard system, because now they do not even have those standards to aim for and to fall back on. If teachers are in the know, then those children are not so bad off, even if the parents have no notion of what the education is about.

But if the teachers are hiding from the world or just out to do their own thing, then heaven help us. In that case, even if the parents expect something special, the children are not only withdrawn but deprived.

The spirit of creativity reaches into all those who intend to benefit from its changing influence. Teachers especially know how they have to allow themselves to be changed, how they have to remain open to the impulse on which the education is based. With standard education it is quite possible to observe a curriculum and remain untouched. The teacher is mostly a facilitator, who at best helps children absorb prescribed information, while at worst he kills off the creative talent and 'creates' problem children. In creative education, such as the Steiner variety, every teacher must him- or herself be creatively predisposed towards the pupils. Then, over a period of time, something special happens. In the absence of such a constantly renewed predisposition, the 'teacher' will become a moral stumbling block.

*

Lastly parents needn't think they can keep an eye on teachers and tell, from outside and from a position of uninvolvement, whether the right thing and the best thing is going on in the school or not. Criticism, no matter how objective, is useless when it comes to creative education.

Only those who are involved in the same spirit can tell where the shoe pinches, if it does, and then they will right away push in the right direction, rather than commenting adversely. When an originally creative educational process becomes hollow, then is the best time for a substantial contribution, by those who notice.

But how can anyone make such a contribution unless he takes the ongoing interest of a learner? A perpetual dialogue and careful conversation is required by those who have a notion of what they want here, if they expect to get beyond fine sentiments and good intentions. Those who have the vision have the task of communicating what they know. Those who do not have the vision have the task of making use of those who do.

* * *

7. Creative transformation in teaching

22/12/'94

The limits we set to what we do in a classroom, as teachers, channel our human resources into something we can call creative transformation, if we intend that the education we make available should be creative and not standard.

A creative teacher responds and reacts inwardly to his pupils while he spends time with them. He experiences them as a group, but also each one individually. He likes or dislikes, he is inclined or disinclined. His inner disposition, his feelings, moods and opinions, while he interacts with those he teaches, is really what we might call his field of operation. How a pupil appeals or occurs to him at any given time and the temporal effect the pupil has on him, in terms of such values as patience, kindliness, equanimity - this is the creative teacher's chief interest, not whether or not information of sorts is imparted or skills for certain performances are acquired. The skills and the information he does not neglect, but his main occupation, continually and repeatedly, and the ongoing focus of his attentiveness, is his changing state of human being.

This changing state of human being is something that by and large begins and ends for him in the classroom. It may also be there for him while he contemplates the progress of his class or of one of his pupils once he has gone home to his supper, but the more proficient-creative teacher manages more successfully to let this context of learning arise in him as he enters the classroom and to subside again as he leaves.

Much could be said about how such a sensibility for the raw materials of creative action first comes about in a teacher, as an organic response to his experience with pupils, but we intend to assume here that he has what it takes and that he is willing to go to some pains to apply what he has. We doubt neither his talent nor his good will. We wish only to describe how he goes about his business and what his ambitions are.

And he does have ambitions. What we called his changing state of human being begins as a very small awareness in him, in fact so small that he has to look for it, often and diligently. And then it gets swamped. Once he has had a glimpse of it however he will never again be happy as a standard teacher, teaching subjects, information and skills alone. Many teachers within the standard system of education are unhappy, confused and disappointed, not to mention downright resentful, because they have not yet taken seriously their real talent for creative teaching. They blame circumstances, the system or themselves, their pupils and colleagues, but they miss the crucial point, which is that they themselves, as human beings, have an inborn longing to teach creatively to which they do not as yet pay heed; or if they do have some notion of it, they try to realize it in a position secondary to their standard teaching, which is a recipe for disappointment, for nerve break-down and early retirement.

*

Once this awareness of his inner state of human being has 'caught', and once he has begun to rely on it, a creative teacher will wish to see it grow in leaps and bounds. He will want to explore it in action, to compare it to that of other creative teachers. He will notice, for example, that in his own case certain elements predominate, such as, for example, impatience and zeal, or lethargy and a certain emptiness of mind. It may be useful for him to identify two or three elements like this that are usual in his case. This will give him something to work with. Then he can observe how he branches out from there. If he notices how often a certain look on some pupils' faces causes him dismay, he marks this down as a fact while refusing to blame either the pupils or himself. Unruly behaviour might be his Achilles heel. His reaction to it must be identified by him. Is it outrage? Is it indignation? Does he feel insulted by it? Does he hate the disturbance, the interruption of standard practices?

Correct identification of his reactions is important. But he has none to identify unless he allows himself to become more sensitive. Sensitivity, on the other hand, implies pain, which can lead to callousness, so that nothing registers. So the identification makes room for further opportunities for him to be touched, to be provoked, to be upset, and worried, and vexed.

The painful, inconvenient motions in himself he should welcome most of all, because with them he can take for granted that his sensitivity is being usefully opened up and widened out. His human being is being alerted and stimulated. The pain will not so readily frighten him into a standard response while he keeps in mind that this is the case. He will suffer the pain gladly because he knows something good is going on. He is becoming a more effective creative teacher.

And certainly he will dismiss from his mind any methods he has learned to do with controlling a class, with 'staying on top' of his pupils, with keeping them in a state of apprehension or such like. While he has any part of his mind on such external checks, he cannot even begin to become alive within, sensitively and intelligently.

*

Once again then, creative education begins with the inward person. But the inward person is individual, made up of natural predispositions, that happily vary from one person to the next. We are, from birth, distinguished, by our talents, our make-up and our reason for being around at this particular time. All of us who work creatively are continually finding out more about this our individuality, about who we are and what we amount to, while we do our work. We should not suppose that any real creativity can be based on self-exploration. Rather during our conscientious interaction with others do we make the true discoveries behind all sorts of doors that were until then closed or not even visible.

So it has to be during his time with his pupils that a creative teacher broadens his outlook and deepens his insights. There is the communal reality of the educational context. The raw materials are a mix of the individualities of teacher and pupils. To look at this, and to identify this mix, and to value it as, in fact, raw materials for creativity, this must be the teacher's initial intention. What we earlier called his changing state of human being, this is the practical registration of these potencies and potentials. Not merely with his calculating eye and sensitive ear does the teacher apprehend this mix of individualities, but with his whole human being does he become increasingly aware of it. His being is the reflector. The question now is, does he act somehow in accordance with what he observes? Does he say to himself: I am experiencing certain sensations or emotions or thoughts which I interpret to mean this, that and the other, so therefore I will behave in the following manner, according to prescribed rules? Of course not. That would take us right back into standard procedure. A creative process combines and unites - marries - subject and object. So we have to come to terms with the fact that the awareness, with one's entire being, of the mix of individualities as raw material - is in itself the second step in the transformation process. This awareness does not allow us to be creative but is itself creative.

And the third step is then, naturally, one's knowledge of this as just stated. While I am aware of what goes on and while I know what it means, I also understand that my knowledge of what it means is effective.

Obviously this can be put in an infinite number of ways, and almost every teacher will feel obliged to put his own stamp on his own creativity. How else can dogma be avoided? But sound doctrine or teaching is of the essence, and such a doctrine of pedagogic creativity is long overdue.

*

A good standard teacher can perhaps afford to become so enthusiastically wrapped up in his subject – to identify himself with the geography he teaches – that this affectively 'rubs off' and pupils become fascinated by geography, (or by the teacher).

However for the standard teacher, his subject is the end and goal of the educational effort he makes. The creative teacher has another goal in view. Certainly there is the 'pretext' of getting together in a classroom and learning something; then there is the 'context' of the subject matter, which is the geography or geometry plus the teacher's attitude towards it and treatment of it. But the 'text' itself is the creative process towards enlightenment. This is not a well-meaning generality or a summation of wishful thinking, but in many particulars a detailed work of ongoing influence with which a creative teacher is conversant and with which he longs to become increasingly familiar.

A good standard teacher says: "My standard approach brings with it that enlightenment in any case. Why make an issue of it?" And if he exists, and if it does, then of course he is right. Creative education cannot have any appeal whatsoever for those who are content with their standard approach.

*

When we use the word 'transformation' we commonly mean a change from one form into another. There is the transformation of image into thought, of thought into feeling, of feeling into being, that sort of thing. The creative transformation we mean in the case of education can be seen as a change from individual nature into human being. The teacher acts as a catalyst and as a facilitator. Due to his presence, the individual mix we mentioned comes about. As a catalyst he activates and stimulates, not by doing but due to being, so that the raw-materials we mentioned come about. He knows that his presence among his pupils has a specific effect. He looks for it and identifies it – in himself, remember, not among or in his pupils. He does not allow himself to draw any conclusions about his pupils. Remember that outwardly he approaches them in terms of spelling, Egyptian culture or the differential calculus, or whatever curriculum has been agreed upon. The transformation process begins with this catalytic stimulus of mutual individuality, which the teacher recognizes and acknowledges in himself, first for what it is and then for what he can do with it. What he does do with it then is covered by the term awareness. He brings into awareness. Not that the raw materials he has to deal with are dead matter. Let's keep in mind that our human natural individuality, at any age, 'wants out', desires to be recognized, longs to be 'raised'. We know from another teaching source that "the son of man must be raised". So in that case, vis-à-vis this mix of individual quantities which 'wishes to come into the light of day', the teacher becomes a facilitator. He eases something into being which he has stimulated into becoming. He makes the path straight for something that might otherwise get caught up in byways and dead-ends. And he does all this, inwardly, while outwardly he discusses aspects of the curriculum.

Even our understanding of the teacher's singular effectiveness as a catalyst depends on our knowledge of your individuality and my individuality striving to become communal, rather than merely existing, inert. This striving in the case of a single individual, child or adult, can be taken for granted by anyone who takes creativity seriously. It's like an unrest in all of us, or like a longing for ease, which, unless true communication takes place, becomes demonic or disease.

Any doctrine of creative education therefore must take into account that children want to grow into mature adults and that all nature intends to come to some spiritual awareness. The 'need to mature' must be taken as given, if I may put it that way. One cannot discuss aberrations of individual nature either unless one is quite consequent about recognizing this need as a fact. It makes a great difference to an educator if he understands that, by definition, human nature, so to speak, plays into his hands. All the same, his hands are indispensable. If he supposes at any time that 'we all grow up in any case', he has lost his way as critically as if he were to insist that it all depends on him. The truth is, that much depends entirely on him, and that we all grow, but not necessarily up.

There is perhaps more to a mature human adult than meets the conventional eye. The very notion of maturity in the case of human beings has to be reviewed every so often. And education has to do with maturation, with the whole business of being brought to the point where we enjoy responsibility for ourselves and others. On the way we learn a few skills and gather some information. What good is a skilful and well-informed brute? What good is a career if the heart is dead? If our brain has no part in our love for one another our brilliance may be awesome though we have no real life. If a teacher has no notion of what it means to be a live human being, the creative process itself will be meaningless to him. He may as well continue to 'educate' to some external standard.

* * *

8. Education as an Art
and
Creative Education

Art is what we do with our various faculties when we make an effort to do it well and when we strive towards excellence. If we ourselves are not properly in tact, our faculties will not operate. This should signal to us that we need to pay attention to ourselves, to our human nature and being. What we often do, by mistake, is pay attention instead to the results of the process in which our faculties fail. This is when artistry sets in. Instead of concentrating on our own inner being, so that our ailing faculties might be refurbished, we try to bring the faulty product up to some standard which has been copied from past perform-ance. Meanwhile we ourselves continue to ail.

This distinction between art and artistry has to be un-derstood. Artistry is an attempt at the correction of a symptom. That makes no sense, because not the symptom should be corrected but the ailment should be cured. If the product of our art is not quite to our liking, we automatically tend to manipulate that product, so that we say: "It should not be like this but like that," and then we have already set up that standard. Art is never according to a standard. Where excellence is attempted, our faculties must be allowed to speak for themselves, so our task is to make this more easy for them. My faculty of speech at this moment is free to behave as it would and I make no attempt to set myself up as a critic or as a judge. I know that my human nature desires to speak for itself, and of course I am interested to learn and to know. My human nature is also yours, and it testifies - or rather it desires to testify - to the humanity in which we all hope to participate. While I give my faculty of speech free reign, as I do at the moment, I make it possible for both you and myself to participate more fully in humanity, and this is certainly a worthwhile achievement. While I do this, and to the extent that I do it, doing perhaps several other things besides which we leave out of question at the moment, I am not an artist but an art worker. I do not comply with an image of what I hope to end up with and I have no idea of any particular result. Certain guidelines or limitations I have laid down for myself make it possible for me, as I adhere to these, to leave my faculty of speech at rest and at peace, which is where I want it. As an art-worker I comply with limitations I have set for myself so that some faculty or faculties should, or rather might, behave spontaneously.

Now where the particular art we have in mind is the education of children or adults, a limitation we must set ourselves is the necessary up-bringing of children, so that our art-education involves this upbringing, and in the case of adults we limit ourselves to immature adults. These limitations are based on our general definition of education as a bringing to maturity. Children are not immature, but they do not grow up to maturity spontaneously, or naturally. Adults may be mature, but if they are immature they may educate themselves, perhaps with the help of a teacher.

These particular limitations lie in human nature itself, and an artful teacher chooses to abide by them, however he sees or feels them, so that his exemplary faculty, his faculty of setting an example, may have free reign and behave spontaneously. Again, every individual teacher is bound to think differently about what it means to set an example, but an example he must set all the same - not by predetermining an image or idea of what should be the case and then attempting - artistically - to meet these or to come up to them by performance according to some standard, but by knowing his faculty of example and letting it come into play. The work he does, if his aim is education as an art, is not directed, therefore, towards the business of setting an example, but towards particular cases and instances of mortification in children and of immaturity in adults. (Mortification is what we call it when a child's upbringing or education has been neglected, just as we call it immaturity when an adult neglects his own mature growth.)

*

Creative education begins from the premise of creation. While art can be described as the natural spontaneity of our faculties, creation involves me and you in person, and in such a way that we become one. This may sound simplistic, but when we look at it more closely it begins to make sense. We are all created unique, and each one of us brings something into the world, due to our birth, that had never before existed and will never exist again.

This you might call our reason for being born. It exists, but potentially, in each one of us. Our reason for existing, from day to day, on the other hand, has to do with the realization of this potentiality. We are at liberty to do this or not to do it. Our happiness is tied into the doing of it. It lies existentially in our interest, therefore, to realized, to make real, that which has come into the world with us. It came into the world with us, and now we may bring it into the light of day, as mature human beings. As children we must be brought up to this. But at the centre of this realization, of this whole business of bringing into the light of day the unique something we were born with, lies the communal, the need to communicate, to get together on it. Creation implies the path from the individual to the communal; creativity presupposes progress from individual expression to personal communication. When we contemplate human beings as creatures we take into account both their development out of a state of being single and their evolution in community. Maturity implies communal activity and being, such as care for others, education and up-bringing of others, though always in a singular way, so that every mature person draws on his own singular individuality during the course of his creative activity. We may imagine it like this: due to our creative action the potential riches of our individual nature become the actual wealth of our personal, communal reality.

The difference between education as an art and creative education is the same, essentially, as that between art and creation. We have to be careful now so as not to assume that creation excludes art, or that art cannot lead to creation. What matters to us at the moment is the proper appreciation of the two as different. If I want to create, I am willing to be changed and I give myself over to certain good influences so that these may be enacted by me or come to pass as events on account of me. There is more to creation than there is to art. Those who are ready to create will not be happy with art in itself. Perhaps they have practiced an art for a while, such as education as an art, but then this insistence on personal commitment and communal engagement makes itself felt in them, almost like an angry dissatisfaction with themselves, or like a miserable disappointment with the way things are going. They miss the totality of self-expression as part and parcel of some recognizable outward scheme of their world. They become moody and fretful. If the nature of the crisis is not correctly identified, time and human substance is wasted with alterations of circumstances and change of activity.

A creative teacher leaves his identity behind as soon as he begins to teach. What counts for him is the change to his human individuality, to the way he is within himself, as he engages with those who want or wish to be taught. He looks forward to being touched by the creative spirit and he makes it his task to be responsible for what happens to the individuality of his pupils. His human being, what he is, he places at the service of immature adults or children. The immature adult must of course wish to be taught; that children want to be taught he takes for granted.

He does not perform for his pupils but he creates freedom for them. His attitude towards the curriculum is slightly different from the attitude of the one who considers his teaching to be an art. Really a creative teacher lets the curriculum take care of itself, and he lets it speak for itself, so that it becomes, as it were, the mere shroud of his activity. In his hands the curriculum becomes the incidental carrier of the various messages he wishes to deliver. His main ambition is not that a pupil should learn to write but that the child, while he learns to write, comes into the possession of a number of good habits of spirit and soul. These habits are the creative teacher's chief concern, and he does not neglect the writing, the spelling and so on.

His colleague, the teacher for whom teaching is an art, approaches the curriculum from the side of performance. It matters to him that the child should do well in terms of the curriculum, but he measures performance by the yardstick of the child's growing-capacity and of the adult's maturing capacity. He does not aim for a union with the pupil but for a full recognition and acknowledgment of him. He says: "This pupil will mature because of the way I introduce him to the world, to human beings and their works." The creative teacher says: "This pupil will mature because I myself am mature."

This lets us know how the emphasis is placed in both cases. For the creative teacher, teaching now and again becomes an art, such as when he undertakes to get to know a pupil in a new or different way. Then he stands back and lets one of his faculties function spontaneously, such as his faculty of imagination, of thought, of speech, of manual dexterity and so on. But he does this not like his colleague, so as to set an example, but in order to offer the pupil greater depth or breadth of experience. He is capable of excellence but uses it as a device.

The teacher for whom education is an art may manage quite well on this basis for long periods of time but then he experiences the limitations of his art detrimentally and risks becoming an artistic teacher, which is to say: someone who manipulates results for their own sake and operates according to an external or internal standard. In order to avoid this he must, on such occasions, take a step towards creativity. So that he may do this more successfully and as soon as possible when the occasion arises, he always nurtures an honourable relationship with his colleague, the creative teacher. Though he cannot fully grasp the sense and meaning of that teacher's pedagogic conduct, he all the same has momentary insights and periodic understanding of it - but only if as a rule he strives to respect his colleague and to honour him, especially at such times as when he feels critical or superior to him. One can understand why he should feel that way, because so much, indeed the main part, of what the creative teacher does cannot be pointed out, cannot be looked at, listened to or talked about.

It helps to distinguish between art and creativity, between art and creation, when it comes to education, simply because, as teachers, we want to know as thoroughly as possible what it is we do, otherwise we do not advance but we regress and our pupils draw the consequences along with us. What do I create, as a creative teacher? Freedom. This means that pupils are both liberated from their mortifications or immaturities and brought into passionate contact with reality. What do I achieve, as a teacher for whom teaching is an art? An excellent example. This means that pupils acquire a taste for freedom and a longing for reality. I myself incorporate this taste and this longing. But taste would end in eating and longing would be stilled as completion. So at least now and again, if not forever after, it falls to me to be creative, and, if possible, to create, otherwise I will stray, from sheer frustration and thwarted passion, into artistry, where I mistake the means for the end and the secondary for the primary.

Education as artistry is a provocation of the pupil and a transfer of dissatisfaction from teacher to pupil. The ailment of artistry is criticism, and where it has taken hold it must be carefully abstracted. Criticism stunts us all in our growth and it leaps from person to person like wild-fire. It corrodes our spirit and undermines our soul. Teachers do well to guard against it, and finally the only way to prevent it altogether is an ongoing concern with the benefits of creation.

* * *

9. Faith and Sense

It certainly helps to be able to say we are certain. But certainty is often no more than an opinion wilfully held. One man sees clearly what for another lies hidden by a fog of disgust. Only look, says the one, you cannot help but agree with me. The other one looks and – shakes his head.

Have we nothing in common, then, on which we can base our agreement about the world? If our senses cannot meet, are we lost, each one, within the isolation of his individuality? Are prejudice and a common fear the only bridge-builders left? When we cringe from an enemy we seem much more likely to lay difference aside and to swallow our pride.

An interesting observation is the following: faith excludes pride. While I have faith I cannot make out that my will conquers yours. If I were to insist on imposing my will on the world I would not be able to see the world clearly because faith would be dead and sensation at loggerheads. By this I mean only that sense cannot function in the absence of faith as caused by pride.

But the world must turn into a shambles for the one without faith. His sense apparatus is merely reflected by it, though he supposes he sees the world as it is.

Now how does faith see the world? With infinite confidence. Faith does not call it the world but world, because the nature of what it sees is endless. Only through the eyes of faith does the infinite scope of world become evident. Then we can cut off our piece from the cake without diminishing the size of the cake. No one is put at risk by your advantage. On the contrary. Whatever you gain is also, by definition, my own gain.

*

World is immense. Only faith has the measure of it, but buried deep inside itself. Is the world then everything I am not? Opinions differ. The word is exchanged, like the word 'reality', as if we agreed on what we meant, but frequently we talk past one another.

56

Faith defines world as the infinite measure of all things, and there we shall let it rest for a moment. Human beings, as we know, are not things, so in accordance with this definition of world by faith, they cannot be part of the world.

Our senses, or rather we as sensible beings, respond to this definition of world by faith as the infinite measure of all things and we say: "Show us what you mean. We believe you, as would seem appropriate, considering that you are faith, but now we would like something for ourselves. We wish to see, hear and touch, and precisely in such a way that nothing is left over for that miserable sister called dissatisfaction." "Ah well," says faith, "there I cannot help you. My business is to supply you with certainty. Why not let that suffice? Accept what I offer as a blessing and you cannot go wrong." "Not enough!" say the senses. "Not enough for us, not to go wrong. We desire to go right! We demand our rights!" "Ah, rights - " sighs faith. "What a pity! But do as you must. What you choose to believe on the basis of my certainty will never disappoint you. You will be blessed with certainty. But if you insist on your rights, well, then you shall also have your wrongs. You pay for the pleasure of being right with a large slice of your certainty, there is no avoiding that." "But" say the senses (not yet taking delight in saying 'but') "is there no way for us to come into our own except by infringing against you? Does faith imply nonsense?" "Of course not," replies faith, a little upset at being so misunderstood. "of course there is a way for you to be perfectly at ease and at peace in your business. Why do you suppose you exist! But that is such a long story, and so long ago forgotten, that I would not have thought you were interested. Whence this sudden desire for knowledge after all these centuries of prejudice and pride? Have you come into a piece of inheritance?"

The senses are acquainted with faith's facetiousness and they take their medicine. This stands them in good stead and right away they are able to express a certain tiredness, a disillusionment with the status quo. They would like to have faith on their side while at the same time ridding themselves once and for all time of every dependency on the world. This makes good sense, and faith livens up when it hears this, because the only sense faith can support is in fact good sense. However, as yet the senses have only just stated their preference. They have not yet mentioned any attitude towards the world that would please them. And naturally faith realizes that a sensible attitude towards the world depends in the end on itself, and on the way it informs the various senses from within. Faith knows what to do but has not yet done it. The senses know what they want but do not know how to get it. In the past, faith has been made to sweat under a burden of apathy and intellectual presumption. There was this faith and that faith but not faith. Children had adhered to it in their wisdom, but youth has no virtue. In terms of faith pure and simple, adults had largely remained immature. They had tried to define faith somehow in terms of the senses. Even by saying that faith contradicted the senses, or that it made no sense, or that it was suprasensible, they still approached it in terms of the senses, from within their sense apparatus, and therefore not faithfully. Such an approach is, of course, impossible. Only he who wishes to have faith has faith, not he who has calculated some content for it which he then tries to swallow and to make others swallow. Devotion, reverence, even holiness, all these were pointless because they operated and existed by appointment, from the direction of faithless sense and applied intellect. The senses themselves were not happy with this arrangement and frequently they complained about problems of stress and strain, about having to appear in a doubtful light and being asked to carry the world on shoulders not at all suited to such a massive task. They did duty in the name of reason without ever meeting the person of that name. They spoke up for virtue and morality because they admired these, but never once were they able to act them out.

*

Knowledge and sense had come to mean the one thing, but faith was not included. No wonder the humanity leaked out of all knowledge. We were all being defined as beings who first had to learn faith, and this of course caused us to overlook that all the time we had it. It was a terrible mix-up. Meanwhile faith held out in caves in the mountains. Today we speak of these mountains as the brain. Our brain holds the secret of simple, single human faith, and if we make ourselves very small and behave not at all boastfully we can make a few very interesting discoveries about faith. Because faith, you see, is the secret of health and happiness. Nowadays this sounds like a boring secret, because everyone knows it. And yet – hardly anyone knows it. Too much is still in that concept of faith that reminds of the churches, of religions, of fanaticism, bigotry and sectarian strife. An unctuous lukewarmness attaches to it, and above all superstition, doltish-mindedness and just plain ignorance. Also weakness and cowardice. Also the sickness of the cult. Indeed what horrors do we not associate with it when we feel challenged in our innermost sense of genuine integrity and self-respect? Reason for a while was the blight of faith and faith the enemy of reason. One wonders today why people bothered with all these dualities and antitheses. Why was faith driven up into the hills? Why was sense deprived of its basis? Why did reason have to walk in a threadbare garment, among those who then turned that attire into a fashion?

Indeed it seems pointless to wonder why. Our time is much better spent if we simply wish to have faith. Very well, momentarily our senses recoil among themselves, but this we can ignore. There is really no need for an analysis of the side-effects that attend an initiation of faith. Again and again we return to the source, which is wishing.

Perhaps we mistake this wish for our will. Perhaps we should first of all be clear about the difference. A wish is no movement of will but a direction of desire. As soon as we decide to desire one thing or another we wish it. Really we cannot desire faith, or desire to have faith, because our head would not be working, our brain would not be in gear. Desire can run loose and then we are in trouble. But in reference to our brain we can point our desire in one direction or another, and then we truly wish. If no desire were involved, then our wishing would be in vain, of course, such as when we speak of wishful thinking, when we delude ourselves about possibilities.

So the wish to have faith and to trust involves desire and draws on the brain. It really amounts to an eminent point of organic concentration.

And of course the implication is, that we have faith and trust in god. However, that 'in god' does not need to be added when we describe what we do here. It goes without saying. It is enough for me to have faith, in order to have faith in god. This is important in the half-light of modern perception, where God, who is a representation of god, is mistaken for god. Our god does not permit representations of himself; illegitimate theology ignores this. When we say that god is spirit, that he is our father and merciful love, this is no image of god but a conscious and wide-awake description of his effect and influence on us. Certainly faith is not god in us trusting himself, because that makes a nonsense of creation, - which is precisely what so many of the so-called faithful seem out to do. Not only do they ignore the creative consequences of faith, such as life from death, but they ensure that their faith is initially defined as devoid of creation.

But sense as based on faith is creative. Creative sense is the automatic consequence of actual faith. Our senses, not as machines but as organs, are world-functional. Take vision for example. Based on faith it brings into physical relationship - and reveals the physical relationship of - our own being with the being of things and persons. My trusting vision of the world reveals it to me as infinitely glorious, and me to myself as involved in that glory. A faithful perception of the cosmos shows it to me as within me as much as without. As soon as an error creeps into that vision I do not blame the world but I look to my faith. This repairs my eye. And on the eye depend all other organs.

Whatever makes good sense is trustingly perceived. I trust the world because it, like myself, is created. That in itself makes good sense. And whether I say body, with its sense and feeling, or mind, with its thought and opinion, it amounts to the same. Not until we wish to have faith do we see that our body and our mind are face and obverse of the one soul. Vision is to our body as thought is to our mind.

In comparison to modern faith, which would set body against mind and spirit against flesh, we would call what we mean here primitive faith. It has always lain dormant in ancient man until one day it surfaced and took on the stature historical. From that day on we knew it existed as a possibility because it challenged our soul. It would not let us rest within striking distance of a world built of faithless sensation.

Next came one who knew the time as advanced, and himself he knew as the bridge to the new time. With his passing began something totally impossible until then, something anticipated proverbially but not realizable until then in the flesh. Contemporaneously it was referred to as the tasting of the truth, and what this meant was that now the senses could be linked organically to human natural faith. It became possible to see, hear and feel faithfully, and therefore, of course, also to think and cerebrate faithfully. I say it became possible. At the same time, and on account of this possibility, faithless vision and thought were now totally at liberty to stray. Hence the great marvels that astounded the world and still astound it today, where not the boastful spirit, but human faith and trust is trodden underfoot.

But faithful vision and thought will always be possible, and even a sense of faith may eventually be developed, for the purpose of a secret communication of the truth. Such a sense of faith ousts modernity by doing violence to it. Modernity is bound by it.

Our chief concern however should be that we look at nothing except what our faith is able to sustain, and that we think nothing except what is able to embody our faith. For some of us that might mean starting from the beginning. For others it implies a period of adjustment.

* * *

10. Faith and Trust

Those who have no outlet for their feelings must be trusted if their emotions are not to turn against them.

An outlet for feelings is a mechanistic notion. It sounds like getting rid of too much pressure. But think of children in the company of immature parents, day in day out, absorbing tensions, calloused by malicious exchanges, having to pretend in order to avoid at least the worst of every conflict.

Emotions are influential. What you say to me while you are possessed by emotions triggers off in me an antithesis of emotion. This tires me out. Finally I crack under the strain. These are conventional expressions to describe individuality at large. My temper flares. Then I hate myself. Something should be settled but I haven't the patience for it, so perhaps I cry out, or inwardly I collapse.

The strenuous work involved in the business of trust requires for its success a simple faith in the continuity of life. Any hindrance to life must right away be recognized as a vehicle to more life.

But emotions and passions especially present such sensational faces that the fascination goes to our heads, so we forget about life because it is not necessarily possessed of a face at all. We like to think of our life as productive but the product is not a sign of life. There may be life that merely awaits our faithful acceptance. In that case it would be foolish to insist on sensation or energy. Faith works with entities that are not patient of sensation, not accessible to energy, and the harder we try to make them out the sillier we feel and look.

When it comes to our brain, we have to ask one simple question: Are we responsible for what goes on there? Are we able to respond, within ourselves, to the numbing pressures that take away all seeming ability to make intellectual progress? Because suddenly the thinking is done elsewhere and otherwise. Gut reactions take over. Let the brain look after itself, we say, when we feel our head as though squeezed in a vice, though meanwhile connections and combinations are easily and gracefully made elsewhere. The world speaks directly to me and I report what it says. I refuse to admit that my brain is not functioning. I may not be using it, but while I report on the world, on the cosmos, on the human universe in its present state and case, my brain lends itself to the task inadvertently, as the organ of plenitude. I am to report on the all, while being part of the all. No wonder that something higher and more far-reaching than my applied brain-power has to come into play. It avails itself of my brain so as to make itself accessible. My brain is the receptor of universal plenitude. I call it the plenum. Within its myriad functions lies this one like the queen bee at the centre of the hive, conscious of only the one thing, that it must be, that it would be, of service.

Moods have absolutely nothing to do with this. My heart at the moment is so far removed from any mood that the very notion of a mood causes me physical pain.

So I must let it work, this brain of mine, in the knowledge that it cannot be forced by me into alignment with my wishes but its duty as world-receptor is holy. If sleep intervenes, I see no reason to prevent it. Only if sleep intervenes too soon I might push back the sense of it and consciously work from the flesh, which is not to be despised. We may work from the flesh while we know it as the bride of good spirit, not torn conscientiously nor abused sacrificially but taken at face value and respected with reverence. Even so long as the elements hold out here we may enter and place our order, so to speak, while the angels minister to us and we become, perhaps, purveyors of beautiful ideas.

Thoughts such as these make no impact on the world for they are themselves imprints of the world. We change nothing about them, only present them as our present state of being allows. We may twist and turn for a while before the onslaught of 'powers and principalities' that 'reside in the air', but we trust that "all shall be well" and "all manner of thing shall be well", and we reject no help. Those who have laboured here have left their mark and we owe them this gratitude. We may even take their work one step further. Again we militate against the forces of sleep and declare ourselves open to the elements. Now we have reached the zone of paternal perfection.

*

Perfection, akin to fulfilment, leaves nothing to be desired. Beyond that, however, there is knowledge of deep-seated satisfaction, which signals optimum growth. We know that within the secret recesses of our being at that moment advantages accumulate and fortunate opportunities are in the planning. The benefits we will reap tomorrow are today being laid up for us. Where? We may say: "in our being," but that only means that by being, and only by being, can we contact these benefits and 'lead them out'. Here we recognize the lovely metaphor of the shepherd, whose voice the sheep know and so they follow him. We say that whatever takes place in our being goes on in secret, but this merely implies that no sensible evidence of it exists, only the knowledge of faith. Secret knowledge, for example, is faith-knowledge, and by being do we consciously access it - or make it happen. We can make only one thing happen, and that is this secret faith-knowledge, which would be brought into the light of day. Only those who know how to be can in fact bring it into the light of day, since for them being is something specific and peculiar.

So we cannot ever make anything happen that we sensibly picture, or imagine, or even think about ahead of time. From the point of view of the truth that sounds absurd but we speak as if it were not. We can bring something like that about, we can cause it, but we cannot make it happen, since something must be quite new for us before it can happen to us. The son of man, for example, (to speak within another frame of reference) comes when we are not looking. But he who knows how to be, makes that happen which lies ready in his being, and in order to understand this we must ourselves be capable of such secret knowledge. If we are not, then we simply take advantage of, and help ourselves to, its being in the light of day and - its being the light of day.

Now here we have much to learn if we feel so inclined. Due to the fact that we who have the choice are, secret or faith-knowledge becomes the light of day. And the light of day is not to be confused with daylight. What we mean here by the light of day is faith-knowledge made manifest. Still it has not become sensible. But what use can it be then for those who have no capacity for knowledge unless it is sensible? Does it make sense to say that they too live in the light of day? Are conditions attached?

They must have faith. Even though their faith is no source of knowledge to them, they must all the same have faith, so that they may have the benefit of the light of day - in which happiness is unavoidable. It comes down to faith and to trust. If happiness is to be permanent, faith must be habitual, so that the manifest light of day may be perceived. Without this fundamental faith, no happy perception. Without this faithful foundation, no perceptive happiness.

What we call the light of day is the revealed secret. It is revealed by those who have faith-knowledge, and any sense knowledge arises from it. Without faith, or trust, our senses are defunct and we might as well talk about life as about a country we have never seen, rather than living. To live means to exist in the light of day, and the light of day is such that our senses take to it and are informed by it. But we are so accustomed to knowing only what we can sense, and at the same time we think of faith only in relation to some Religion, of trust only in response to what we have first judged to be trustworthy, that we find ourselves trapped in a corner.

So in order to learn of the light of day we try to activate our ... shall we call it our faith and trust potential? Perhaps if we think of it as an ordinary human faculty first, and only then as the fundamental human faculty, we will have more success. A marvel worth considering is that <u>to wish to have faith is to have faith</u>. There is no gap of function between the wish to trust and actual trust. Another thing worth keeping in mind is that we may not have any evidence of the fact in itself that we trust, but there is the related experience of various crippling inhibitions gradually fading and disappearing altogether.

So wish to trust and know that now you trust. And of course do take time with it. It takes time to acquire a good habit, especially if thereby we need to replace one or two bad ones. Even if you were to take only ten minutes every morning to practice faith there would be immeasurable gain for you. Wish to trust and know that even then you trust, and keep that up for the time it would take you to jog around the block or to watch a short television program. Your next step would be to do it during the day while you are doing other things. Faith does not interfere with the sensible business of the day. On the contrary, that business becomes much more sensible. And nonsense will stop. Wish to trust and do not look for any sign that you are trusting. Your less than sensible activities will begin to seem less crucial. They were only your untrusting, suspicious senses running amok. Your organic being thrives on faith and disintegrates without it. All of your organs must have this input of trust or else they become impaired.

That you wish to trust, this is of course the main thing. You may well say: If I have no notion of it, how can I wish it? But I say to you: you do have a notion of it. It may be covered by prejudice and overlaid with false learning and spoiled by absurd experience but you have it within you to trust. Naturally no one can make you do it. You are perfectly at liberty to go to ruin. But you will be a stumbling-block to those around you. And eventually your light will go out.

We can learn trust from children. In them this faculty is at least not abused yet by the wilful adultery open only to adults. Perhaps that in their presence, if you look for it, you may come face to face with what you are missing.

Those who have a faith usually have the least faith. To have a faith means to have a head full of particular notions, commonly concerning some aspect of supernatural divinity, and such intellectualized mystifications can only put a blight on our organ of faith. So as we learn to have faith, we discover how lively and sensible a thing this is compared to having a faith.

Not that faith is sensible, but having faith, and trusting, is eminently sensible. Where trust is our grounding, real sensibility can take root and there will be no more separation of the sensuous from the sensual, which is such a. common impairment of human being.

Then it makes sense to ask myself now and again: Have I faith right now? Do I trust at this moment? Human beings are to have their hands on the controls of the universe, no wonder they have so much to lose in this department. We know nothing of value about human beings if we do not take into consideration this unique faculty of ours, and the way all our other faculties depend on it. If I cannot say: Yes, now at this moment I trust - I should right away wish to do so, otherwise I am missing out and selling myself short in some department. And if preaching such as this does not make you at least a little bit angry, your trust is either thorough and your faith perfect - or blind.

* * *

11. Fully Human Wisdom

We listen in, while the spirits of the age whisper: "Self-gratification – self-gratification" We know nothing of these spirits while we mind our own business as servants of life. We are and we do. "Let me be and let me do," we say righteously, "and do not ask me to believe in anything because it sickens me to the heart to be constrained in my heart, where freedom constantly seeks expression."

Meanwhile the spirits of the age listen in and are beset by jealousy. What have they not, that we have, and they are enticed by it? Something about us attracts them and draws them within the circle of our consciousness, so that we become almost passionate in our rejection of such a thing as these spirits. We insist they do not exist because we do, and our insistence becomes adamant, heated - rebellious. And all the while these spirits move into us and avail themselves, by subtle invasion, of our utmost will and desire. What we reject, after all, is not them, but our own clever representations of them. They themselves are the essence of our rejection.

What does it mean to be possessed by these spirits? Quite simply it means that we cannot become our own

70

true being. We cannot become what we are and who we are. We are more like puppets who suppose themselves free than like free human beings. We energize our every move with thoughts of a self-will and a self-desire, and yet this self which we admire and prize is the sum-total of all these spirits of the age claiming us for themselves, for their vehicles and embodiments.

For spirits have no greater aim than to be in the daylight. A sudden outburst of temper, a show of supreme indifference, an articulate expression of pretence, a series of morbid complaints, a chronic unsteadiness of purpose: - these are all subtle manifestations of these spirits. These are ways in which these spirits gratify themselves. They like nothing better than a juicy belief- system before which the children of man prostrate themselves and do homage - to a God who is energized by self-gratification. Such a God has the nerve then to cheapen his subjects by subjecting them to always just sufficient insecurity so that others must be drawn into the circle. Satisfaction shall be flaunted so as to arouse an envious imitation. Ease shall be boasted of, so that others should feel ashamed of their natural human affliction. Comfort shall be displayed so as to create in others a secret jealous rage. The envy, the shame; the resentment and rage - in these, and as these, the spirits of the age are empowered by us, even while we seem to ourselves to be so firmly rejecting them. Our rejection of the idea of these spirits amounts to an acceptance of their reality.

As soon as we understand this, something remarkable can happen. As soon as we wonder if this might in fact be the case, we find stirring in ourselves a human natural instinct. I do not say: an instinct for this of for that, but: a human natural instinct and something like an element of integrity before the world. Whoever discovers this element of integrity in himself is not any more awed or overwhelmed by the massive images of the world but he quietly goes his way, not caring much any more what is said or thought about him among people. He is and he does, and he knows now that this is what counts. He knows it. Such knowledge is a blessing. Such knowledge is happiness incarnate. Whoever has such knowledge is protected against the spirits of the age in the sense that for him they simply cannot exist. In him they can find no hold, no persuasive substance - no energy to glut themselves.

*

What nonsense, to speak of these 'spirits of the age'! What fairytale monsters are these, to have acquired such a hold over our imagination that we serve them by refusing to accredit their existence and we are enslaved by them as soon as we believe in them? Can anyone help us escape from this maze?

What we believe in makes us or breaks us. Believe in these spirits and soon they take hold of your being and shape it. Belief-systems are set up so that you will believe in these spirits. Today literally hundreds of these systems make the rounds. All can be boiled down to the spirits of the age, dressed up in one way or another. Then it may happen that a man says: "Enough is enough! Henceforth I believe in nothing!" Little does he realize how far he is ahead of those who believe in something they imagine. Holding on to your money is better than investing it in swampland for real estate. As soon as you accredit the products of your imagination you are standing on a bog with a trowel in your hand. And those spirits of the age are products of our imagination. We do well to withdraw our imagination so that it might be distinct. Our distinct imagination is wonderfully creative. Its function is mythic. Myth is the lifeblood of all of our experience. Experience withers, our senses die, the world becomes a shadow-land, if we let our imagination run riot - or - harness it to a belief. Beliefs eventually topple under their own weight. Those who are tied to them perish beneath them.

"I just am and do." Such a person does not believe in any thing but such a person believes in god. Her being is the being of god. Along with a great mystic such a person might say: "I am god," while certainly not meaning: "I am God." An individual who says: "I am God," should right away be stripped of his credentials because such a one is likely to commit mass-murder or to seduce millions into insanity. But to be god is simply to recognize that one's being is one with the being of all. Among the insane, one is smart not to say that, because god sounds like God, and the dead cannot, in any case, distinguish between the upper and the lower case. They know only the one all-embracing monster that usurps their being and renders them monstrous, while persuading them that they are good.

"I only am and do, and I believe in nothing," says the one who has experienced within herself that kernel of human integrity which will not permit a commitment to cheap consolation or to false ease. "I envy those who have their God, because they have it so easy!" This is only another way of saying: "If the choice is between false ease and real hardship, give me hardship," - with the secret conjoiner: "If only I had true ease!"

In order to be in the possession of true ease, we must know that all the spirits of the age are defeated. They exist, these spirits, that goes without saying, but their existence is a fog, while our integrity is the sun that blasts it. Believe in these spirits and the fog becomes spectral; fear or respect those spectres and they begin to seem real. We base our own existence on them and they support us with all the strength of a worm-eaten floor joist.

Much better to 'just be and do'.

Alas, there is more, much more in the offing! That kernel of human integrity, that instinct for the truth, is nothing dead. It operates, like the proverbial yeast in the loaf.

*

A whole new awareness is required to take account of this inward, organic operation. A kind of restlessness signals its presence. If this restlessness is misunderstood, there can be much waste. So first it must be actually noticed, identified and then accepted as something that takes time; its own sweet time. Imagine the baker who dumps the loaves because the dough rises! Our own intelligent awareness of this yeast process in ourselves is an aspect of the whole operation. This is what makes this particular awareness so unique, and something more than consciousness. Those who insist on consciousness, vis-à-vis some reality that is either subjective or objective, prevent that awareness in themselves. Within such organic awareness object and subject coincide. The experience of this allows someone to say: "I am god", meaning: "I cannot differentiate between my own being and god's being." Imagine a drop of rainwater falling into the ocean.

This business of this peculiar restlessness steeped in this unique awareness is especially important nowadays, because of two phenomena that play into almost every aspect of modern life. One is the anxiety to which we fall prey, accidentally and automatically, due to being modern. This anxiety seems like that productive restlessness, but in fact is nothing like it. It does not stem from integrity but amounts to a lack of trust, so that it must be dealt with, or rather confronted by, trust. The other phenomenon does not start inside us, as anxiety, but outside, as hypocrisy, where we have neglected to guard ourselves against the influence of those who preach the standards of mere appearances, morally, religiously and even charismatically, so that we become uncertain and insecure, straying from one therapy to the next, paying for bread and receiving plastic. This hypocrisy can be bought in a multitude of books and courses and discipleships which all have the one effect, that they undermine our character and spoil our chances of ever acquiring any human integrity. Such a mania or craze may again, like the anxiety, be mistaken for that productive restlessness of which we would wish to be aware, but neither trust nor awareness can help us here because we are literally addicted to a falsehood and attached to a destructive pleasure, such as a conceit of tyranny or an affectation of slavery. Only one thing can save us, and that is an earnest search for the personal truth.

Which brings us back to that kernel of human integrity organically operating within us and giving evidence of itself as restlessness that responds favourably to awareness and then - the result is a product or a certain productivity.

We become beneficially effective, though often and again not right away in a manner we ourselves or others openly recognize. For example, our presence alone may serve, while we still suppose we must shift and alter so as to justify our presence. Conscience can pose a problem. A social conscience was perhaps formed in us as an acquired habit of seeing the world and ourselves through the eyes of people and not through our own eyes, which we are now beginning to trust. So we have to learn to think for ourselves, conscientiously and with consequence and above all responsibly, in the knowledge that I myself and only I can come up with solutions to certain problems which only I seem to recognize.

Once I have learned that even by being I do, I can even afford to do, because now I am less likely to mistake that productive restlessness in myself for a need for mere action, for business and commotion.

Before real action must come an experience of rest, so that action may proceed out of this rest, and not amount to an expression of restlessness. The one who says: "I am" is at rest and he who is at rest truly is. That is not action which merely dissipates nervous energy. All that nervous energy is best repressed until we have once again established within ourselves our recognition of the fact that we are, not in hiding from others, in some private space where only morbidity can grow, but here in the light of day, ordinarily preoccupied with the problems of the day.

*

This, then, is a creatively practical response to contemporary issues and concerns in the light of the wisdom that is not merely human but fully human. This wisdom is not based on any beliefs and does not categorize opinion, but it springs human naturally where room is made for it and where suitable ethical and communal conditions are created for it.

* * *

12. How to admit Guilt

Guilt is not something we feel unless all of our human being is under attack. Only those who have human being, only those who are in the possession of this precious commodity, can feel guilt, and therefore this feeling should be viewed as a mark of distinction.

Or approach the topic from the other side and recognize that we cannot, in ourselves, know of any such thing as guilt unless the good, or god, has moved into our life and has begun to motivate our actions. In comparison to that movement and motivation then we feel guilt. Naturally that feeling should therefore be accepted, then, as a harbinger of the good, or as a messenger of god.

Guilt must therefore, right away upon experience, be properly identified and rightly understood. In itself, guilt is a sensation of evil. But it cannot be a true sensation. The evil has distorted our sense, and now it's up to us to recognize that distortion. We have to think and learn about it at a time such as while we are not under the sway of guilt and forced hack into ourselves, full of idiotic notions as to the cause of our guilt and as to all sorts of criticism and condemnation.

While we feel guilt, we are in a sense condemned, and we do well indeed not to wonder at all whether we are justly or unjustly condemned. Let us simply admit to ourselves that since we feel guilt, there must be within us a receptivity for the good. Now this is in fact what we have to admit to ourselves, right physically, with mind and body, and our doing so actually constitutes a reception of the good before which we initially felt guilty. Obviously we felt guilty because something within us was not as manly as it might have been, but what this was should not concern us. Such concern only confuses the issue for us. What should really matter to us is that something more manly is on offer for us, and that now is the time to behave in a way that will bring us post haste into the possession of it.

*

Let's be more specific now about how to behave in the face of the guilt we feel if we want to take the best possible advantage of it.

Consider what the difference may be between you saying to yourself: "I feel guilty", and saying: "I am guilty". Look at the latter first. Guilt has to do with our moral or spiritual being, just as a debt pertains to our financial situation. But be careful, because the comparison can only be made to the extent that the realm of appearances is a reflection and a reminder of our inward reality. Guilt is, then, like a debt, and if you are guilty, you owe something. But you do not owe it in the eyes of people. Therefore, the notion that being guilty implies something else now called punishment is a confusion of appearance with substance, because, where punishment does come into it, is not as in the popular realm, where a man is convicted of stealing and then punished with a prison sentence, but as the feeling of guilt, which is intended, as a punishment, to work in our favour. Of course, ideally a spell in a penitentiary is supposed to make a guilty man penitent, and if he understood his punishment as it might happily be understood, he would set out on his prison term with a song on his lips, because he would say to himself: "I have made a stupid mistake by stealing something and my term in goal will give me ample time to take myself to task and to work towards my moral regeneration." If instead he says: "Damnit, I've been caught, now I have to put up with this inconvenience," he gains nothing and will probably repeat his mistake.

In the moral realm, when we look at it as somehow distinct from the popular realm of appearances (which is a sensible enough thing to do for the sake of increased understanding) we are guilty and owe something only in the sense that some substantial life value is being held out to us at that moment, such as for example eternal life itself, and our guilt consists in our comparison to that. This only makes sense while we view ourselves correctly as beings that grow and evolve. A plant grows towards the light. The sun shines on the plant in the morning, and first thing in the morning the reaction of that plant to the greater light might be a guilty one. The plant is guilty until it responds gratefully to the light, stretching itself, opening leaves and petals, and so on. Only until the plant actually responds to the new light and to additional light, and only while it ignores the feeling of guilt, that is to say: its own comparative state of darkness, can it be said to be guilty. Of what is it guilty during that time? Of not yet responding, for its own sake, to the blessing of more light. What does it owe and to whom does it owe it? It owes a light-oriented response to itself as a growing being. And what is its punishment for not yet responding?

Nothing else except that feeling of guilt, which can at a moment's notice be 'suffered' and rightly understood not as a hateful inconvenience but as an encouragement to respond creatively by stretching towards the new light. If this plant were a perverse, morbid and superstitious little plant, it would turn even further away from the light, or insist on not responding, or get tangled up in materialistic arguments about morality in reference to weeds, gravity, moisture, cutworms and frost, and it would naturally become more guilty like that, and wallow in its guilt, and then get stepped on. Good. That's what it deserved. We all get stepped on when we behave like that. We are ungrateful for the light and persist in ignorance of what guilt and punishment are all about, not to mention the difference between being and feeling guilty.

*

The man who knows what he is about will wisely assume that as an evolving adult human being he is always in the presence of endless good, in comparison to which he himself is always like one who reaches out and takes, for others and for himself at once. If suddenly he feels guilty, he realizes that there is something more specific to be gained, in that particular area of his being where he feels guilty. His work becomes for a while more specific, in the face of that feeling. It suffices for him that he feels guilty, he doesn't have to wait until he actually is guilty on account of neglecting to act on that feeling.

First comes the feeling of guilt. That is the signal: "Here is an open door through which you may step into greater and more life."

Now let's talk about how we step through.

The topic is: How to admit guilt. It should be obvious by now how this can even become problematic. Where does the admission come in? Once I have allowed myself to be taught about the nature of guilt and once I have taken the trouble to learn the difference between feeling guilty and being guilty - then I have to take the time to apply this knowledge to my own experience and keep in mind what I have learned while I experience guilt and all the attendant feelings and thoughts relating to shame, self-recrimination, rebellion, punishment, accusation and self-justification: the list is endless. I have to be aware of what I know on one hand and of what I am going through on the other side (sic). That is work. I hold on to what I know and believe, and I act in accordance with it while I suffer all those unpleasant experiences. That is what I do if I want to get ahead and not get stuck. My suffering of the feeling of guilt etc. should be cheerful and glad, after all, eh? - because don't I know what is coming my way? Don't I know that the guilt is a sign of more approaching life? Then let me act like it; let me suffer cheerfully, in the full knowledge of why I'm suffering. If the painful feeling of guilt suddenly flips away from me so that I couldn't suffer if I tried, then let me quietly remember that the feeling of guilt is not necessary before I can set out to – admit my want.

Admit my what? My want of life. In relation to what is available I always want life. I mention this, because our approach to guilt can be thwarted in that suddenly some-thing like high spirits whisks the whole situation away from us so that we end up saying to ourselves: "What is all this nonsense about guilt, after all? What have I to be guilty about?" That is a trick that is being played on us, and we do well to have a second arrow in our quiver. This second arrow is the knowledge that we can always do with more life, and that if we don't feel that we want it - we want it nonetheless. Those who impregnate their mind with this knowledge become unconquerable. Not only do they not need to wait until they feel guilty before they act wisely, but they can actually act wisely even when they notice themselves feeling full of themselves, beyond all improvement and correction. This kind of arrogant presumptuousness is perhaps even more dangerous than guilt indulged in, because it amounts to self indulged in. Our knowledge about the nature of guilt should be backed up by this knowledge about self-satisfaction masquerading as innocence.

Simplify the whole thing. Admit, more life is available than you have. Know that this life is forever pressing in on you. Then admit that life.

You feel guilty? Admit that feeling to your suffering self. Get rid of all these childish notions of being able to shake off your burden by confessing this guilt. Learn how to carry your burden and know guilt for what it is.

You suppose you must be a bad person because you feel guilt? Don't kid yourself. The worst persons don't feel any guilt. You suppose by confessing an error - given you could identify it - you might re-establish your innocence? Don't kid yourself. No one is innocent, especially not those who feel innocent. Personally I would much rather feel guilty than innocent. The path from guilt to life is more straightforward and less deceptive than the path from innocence to life.

*

Sober attentiveness, persistent application - this is what is wanted, for all our sake. Let him who feels guilty rejoice. It clears the mind something wonderful. The feeling of guilt is a merciful reminder, a magnanimous indication, a valuable sign. You want to admit guilt? What would that mean, now?

We could join a club of the guilty. Here we are, fellow sinners, we are all guilty and we feel it, so let's admit it to one another, woe are we. Let's invent misdemeanours to explain these feelings of guilt and let's vie with one another, who can be the guiltiest of all, because now that we are all wallowing in the same mud, isn't 'life' so much more interesting? Let's discuss sin, and original sin, and cardinal and venial sin. What fun! What, have we forgotten the most exciting of all: mortal sin? Now there's an indulgence! Imagine being able to sin in such a way that ...etc. etc. Next week for our AGM we will invite a speaker on the delicious topic of Mortal Sin and Eternal Punishment. Then we will get together for our usual social evening with all those who have laughed loudest at these witticisms, in their innocence, because they are so close to our heart and they know it. We would have joined with these superior innocents before now, and indeed we have enjoyed many workshops with them, but something stands in the way of a common institution. At the end a squabble breaks out over the label: should we call ourselves Liberal Perverts or Perverse Liberals? Experts are working on a Unified Field Theory. VIP's sit yearly in congress to labour towards a single World Church. This problem of the label remains.

Isn't it strange, finally, that none of this is open, really, to argument or discussion. Either one accepts or one doesn't. Either one applies or one doesn't. Either one goes down this road or one doesn't. Those who insist that their guilt should mislead them have their reward. In the short term that might seem more pleasant. Those who insist that guilt should be felt as an indication of badness or of evil, which evil should then be removed, will never be free. While guilt assails them, they will invent ever new evils to be exorcised, and in the absence of guilty feeling they will feel superior and be useless.

While we confuse guilt with evil, we are of course reluctant to admit, to ourselves or to others, that we do feel guilt, because we suppose such an admission will cast us into a bad light. Then, finally, we admit the guilt, but what we really admit is how evil we have been - which is clearly not right, no matter how emotional or enthusiastic or sentimental we feel while we do it.

The thing that might be worth admitting, in the sense of a confession, is our entirely misguided notion of guilt and guilty feelings. That would certainly let in (admit) some new light for us, so that we might then relate to others how it came about, in our own peculiar case, that we gained freedom from guilt and a lease on new life. But you cannot wait, before you admit your error in this department, until you feel guilty about it. That time will never come. We must mend our way on account of insight into a better way, not by punishing the one we suspect of making our way crooked, even if we suppose we ourselves are to blame. Without the one who came, and on which account we felt blame, we remain the same.

* * *

13. How to measure success
in creative education

Creativity has become a fashionable word. Consensus seems to have it, that a creative person makes things happen. What it is that happens has to be looked at separately. Another kind of creativity is linked from the outset to values such as moral values. If we think of it as part of the definition of a creative person that there is access to power, then we might ask: is this power available to the person no matter what his intention, or does it increase and decrease in accordance with his intention being good or not so good? We can go on then to realize that 'good' to one person is whatever pleases him, to another whatever he has achieved, and to a third whatever comes from god. The first one measures success by his senses, the second by his judgment. But the third has moved on into a different sphere of measurement altogether. He has a personal experience of the good and he knows it to be self-evident. Obviously he would find it as impossible to argue that experience away as another man his experience of a train rushing along tracks, or of the difference between a just and an unjust law. This difference can be demonstrated, logically, just as the train can be described, accurately. But, the good can only be shown, by personal example. In the case of the good, not my senses or my ego, but I myself have moved into the foreground and into the light, of day. There is no hiding from a good example. One is either open to it or not. Where the good is concerned, power falls into line with such values as kindliness, meekness and mildness, above all with mercy. Be merciful and you cannot fail to do good. Kindliness and mercy are truly powerful, whereas force and energy are apparently but not in reality powerful.

Creativity that is not just fashionable and popular is mercifully powerful and good. If we are truly creative we do good. And since all experience of the good is self-evident, we should not expect to be able to measure it from any other point of vantage. Only from within any creative process, or at least in empathy with it, can we appreciate what goes on and appraise that it goes on. Appreciation and appraisal are therefore our 'standards' of creativity. Where something good is going on, appreciation and appraisal will find it out and will right away support it. Judgment will veil it, criticism will block it out.

This is very important. We have to differentiate clearly here between two things and we have to make an effort to understand each one separately as far as possible and as much as we can, because eventually we are going to see them come together, as an articulate whole and as a workable unit. Certainly it would be possible to discuss creative education entirely as an impulse, as something that is real in itself, whether we respond to it or not. I have done that at length elsewhere. The emphasis there is on the individuality of the pupil or student, on the educational intention of the adult as teacher, and on the quality and progress of the personal relationship between pupil and teacher, student and instructor, and so on. The present enquiry as to any success measurement of such education would seem to focus our attention more particularly on something like an applicability of certain ideals within a conventional, less than ideal state of affairs that is considered to hold sway in our day.

But this is only half true. I expect to lose the good will of most readers as soon as I explain why. Creative education is not an ideal. It is a reality. We can lay hands on it. At he same time, the conventional state of affairs is in fact ideal, but in the special, as yet unconventional sense of 'striving towards ideals' 'falling short of the ideal', 'seen in relation to an ideal' and so on. Creative education, however, has nothing to do with the realization of ideals, or of 'the ideal', whatever that is. It has to do with reality being made manifest. It has to do with bringing something that is ready within human beings to awareness.

The most usual type of education on offer in Britain, Europe and many other countries, is something I call, in comparison to creative education, standard education. An idea of the human being and of his role in society underlies this education. The attitude towards knowledge is quite different. Knowledge itself is not at all the same thing in both cases. Education to a standard exclusively involves knowledge of things we can point at and point out to one another. I use this term 'point at' in its broadest sense. I mean what we look at, listen to and think about. We could also call it the knowledge of appearances. No reference at all is made to anything that lies outside this sphere; on the contrary, pains are taken to avoid it. The name that is given to the thing that is being avoided usually reflects the type of risk one supposes is being presented to a satisfactory achievement of the standard. A proponent of standard education literally has no idea of creative education, and since he must work with ideas, nothing else should, in all fairness, be expected of him. This simple truth is all too often ignored. There is no way of making standard education somewhat more creative. Those who speak about creative education as if this could be done do it the worst disservice. If I want to teach a child a simple skill, such as map reading, I can perhaps bring him up to a certain standard of map reading within a certain time. Perhaps. If he actually wants to acquire that skill, I have a fairly good chance of succeeding. If it's all the same to him whether he learns this or not, I can try to make the possession of this skill attractive to him, I can woo his attention, hold out a reward for him and threaten him with punishment. I might awaken in him an interest, or a repugnance, depending on how I go about it. We call a standard teacher good if he knows how to do what he intends to pass on, if he combines firmness with kindness, discipline with cheerfulness, and that sort of thing. He won't hold the opinion that map reading makes someone a better person, but he cares about the difference between skill and ineptitude, and he prefers the latter. If someone has hired him, for pay, to teach that child map reading, this complicates matters somewhat, because he feels different now about whether he fails or succeeds than if the individual he attempts to teach had initially come to him and shown an interest. However all this still has to do with standard education, whether it's poorly or well done, for money or for love, in response to the pupil's request of to satisfy either the pupil's parent or the requirements of the law as defined by the government of that country.

And progress in map reading can be measured. Any one of a number of external standards of measurement can be applied. Various interpretations can be put on results achieved or not achieved. Really standard education is more like training than anything else. Our mind is trained. Our body, even our soul can be trained. It's a useful thing to do and it can be underdone or overdone. Too little training leaves faculties dormant. Too much training strains and exhaust the faculties or can cripple them for life.

The next consideration is the spirit in which standard education or training is pursued. There is the spirit of independence which tries to make everyone self-sufficient. There is the spirit of excellence and competition, which can serve or become a thing in itself. A vainglorious spirit amasses a wealth of knowledge while the human being remains impoverished. A noble spirit would train us in skills to be of service to our fellow man. Such an education contributes to a healthy society in a community that is sure of its values. Each of these spirits imposes its own system of evaluation and quality gradation. Through time, different spirits rise to the fore, are supported or combated, incarnated of dispensed with.

Standard education always aims at the faculties of the person to be educated. Good standard education or training aims at the development of these faculties while keeping the sanctity or integrity of the person in mind. Bad standard education ignores this and treats a person, no matter how young or old, as nothing in addition to a set of faculties that can be developed. In other words, it depersonalizes. Gradually the very capacity for personhood, for communicating with others in a truly meaningful way, is eroded and allowed to fall into neglect. The depersonalized faculty is a mechanism. People are turned into mechanisms. The degree of their mechanistic development can still be accurately measured, by external standards. It can be tested and graded like all standard results. As people allow themselves to be turned more and more into mechanisms they will of course search for more ego-flattering interpretations of these measurements. Where personhood is left hollow, a balloon of creditable degrees is substituted, and so on, to a great height of absurdity.

The desire for creative education is like a reaction to this absurdity. Suddenly one realizes what has been going on for some time and is appalled. A few responsible adults appear on the scene who are gifted with a discerning spirit, and with a discernment for spirits. The emphasis is taken entirely away from faculties that are to function in a particular way and is placed on the person, and on the individual traits that make for personality. The human being is redefined. He is no longer a bundle of processes and a capacity for potential performances but a select being with a desire or wish to become aware of himself and of the world in freedom. One assumes one is born with such a longing. Then one notices how this natural growth impulse is everywhere thwarted and one begins to cogitate about how one might assist it in overcoming these hindrances and handicaps, how one might go about lending it confidence and helping it gain in strength. A disposition of insight and care develops that deserves to be called creative. An adult looks at a child, or, for that matter, at another adult, and sees a frustrated soul, a disappointed spirit, an under- or over-nourished body. He sees an appetite for mystery and wonder, a craving for a knowledge that aids and abets growth, a longing to understand in such a way that more life becomes available rather than that death becomes less of an affront. He sees a problematic psyche and discovers in himself via compassion and pity a spontaneity of solution. He approves, appraises and appreciates and makes himself available chiefly as a person who sets an example of awareness of the world and of himself.

This personal example is the main aim and goal of the creative educator. Whatever his pupils do or however they behave, he returns again and again to the working personal example he sets them. For he knows that by this example he draws them out of themselves and returns them to themselves, in short, he educates them, creatively.

*

Right away we ought to ask: How does the creative educator 'measure' the quantity and quality of his own, personal example? Because, let's face it, this is principally where measurement comes into its own in this case. There is no external standard whatsoever and such a thing as an internal standard would have to be talked about at length before we would feel alright about committing ourselves to such a notion. The teacher does not 'test' his pupils, but he is himself tested, in terms of his relationships to his pupils. What he measures is something like his response or reaction to them. This means, of course, that he has to have at his fingertips a body of knowledge that allows him to handle such reactions and responses. When he feels anger rising within himself, he does not simply suppress it, for example, for the sake of an appearance of equanimity, outwardly to his pupils and inwardly to himself, but he transforms it. This is a creative act, and it constitutes the sort of thing that allows us to speak of this education as creative in the first place. If the teacher experiences indifference, this is another valuable, measurable quantity for him. He may even thoroughly dislike his pupils, or one in particular, or, what amounts to the same from this creative point of view, he may like one too much. Right away he takes stock of that, and he notices it sooner rather that later, as a simple fact. He continually trains himself in an increasing awareness of such facts, so that the creative transformation can be worked by him. He begins by measuring. He continually strives to retain and regain the measure of himself - that would be a way of putting it. We have mentioned only anger and indifference. When creative teachers get together they do not discuss pupils so much as their own factual responses to pupils, so that they can then help one another in upgrading these responses. "John makes me impatient!" is a tacit confession of a momentary failure by a teacher. "I feel impatient in the presence of John," is either a complaint or a statement of fact leading to a creative act of transformation. If it is perceived, by another teacher, as a complaint, then compassion is required to help re-establish a medium of creativity. While the teacher blames the pupil for the impatience he is on the wrong track. If he blames himself, it must be the sort of intelligent blame that leads to adult responsibility, in the knowledge that forgiveness is part of the fibre of our real experience as we live and work with one another.

*

Now needless to say, the measuring the teacher does in terms of his inner creativity is not the same as the measurement in relation to standards. The creative teacher does spelling, long division and map reading with his pupils, but for him, success at these is not his real or main purpose. These activities for him are means to a greater end, namely the ever growing and enriching awareness of oneself and the world. To a standard teacher such awareness is either an empty word, or something that 'comes along anyhow, doesn't it?' We have to face the perhaps painful fact, that any creative teacher has an insight into something of which even a good standard teacher knows nothing; or if he has had a glimpse of it, he makes no special effort to let it become a part of his educative impulse, not to mention making it the chief part.

How, then, does a creative teacher measure success, specifically? Initially he measures his own success in overcoming his setbacks and repairing his shortcomings. He sees himself as a learner, and knows that he fails as soon as he stops learning. The success of his pupils is organically wrapped up in his own. They cannot help but rise to any occasion to which he rises. Certainly he does not judge their growth, or estimate the state of their souls, or any such thing. His own inner liveliness forbids that. How could he say that a pupil fails?

He can only admit that he has failed the pupil. And if necessary, he will admit this gladly. Even a failure in creativity is greater than a success to a standard. As for the measurement of the standards, this the creative teacher pursues in the ordinary way, only that he places different interpretation on the results. In a way every individual pupil has to be set his own standard, and this in accordance with the teacher's perception of the pupil's organic development and growth. Such standards are, of course, of secondary importance and of a subsidiary nature. Practice shows what one would expect, namely, that creatively educated children do better at reading, writing and arithmetic.

93

Which brings us to an important side-issue. Creative education is not the norm. It has to be somehow fitted into the system of standard education these days. Often a hybrid approach results. The pressure on those who understand and therefore favour creative education becomes almost unbearable at times, as one tries to survive. The ensuing struggle must be viewed in a positive light by creative educators. One does not adopt creative education like yet another method, but one grows into it precisely under pressure. Under the pressure of all that seems against us, and by welcoming that pressure, we must define and redefine our purpose, widen our horizons, deepen our insights and vary our approaches. There must be an ongoing dialogue among those in the know. Only by living example, not through any kind of well-meaning evangelism, can progress be made, so that teachers and pupils - more than succeed.

While nations exist, national school systems will exist - to support the nation. State education is education for the benefit of the state, not for the wellbeing of the pupil. A political state that supports creative education is either enlightened indeed and also has the good fortune of an example of creative education that is worth its salt to observe - or else it is too tired and lazy to care about the difference. In an unenlightened state, the depersonalization of the population by bad standard education has progressed so far that the mechanistic skills to be acquired and the amount of dead and silly information to be 'absorbed' has increased to such an absurd degree –evidently as an-ill-conceived attempt to make up for lost ground – that creative educators have to set a limit and redefine even the curriculum. Theirs can then become a lonely task. The charge of 'not measuring up' will invariably be levelled at them.

They must accept this as a compliment, without seeming to do so. In the case of countries where centralized external control and measurement has nearly 'taken over' in the attempt to 'improve education', creative educators will understandably be tempted to keep their distance, wherever possible, from state influence. Where funding becomes a problem, an extra dimension is added to the creative educational impulse, because now one must ask oneself: will funds not perhaps come along, somehow, as some kind of a measure of the school's success? This is a ticklish question, because all too readily trivialized. Certainly how a creative school holds out and how it behaves during a serious financial pinch is a measure of its strength. Perhaps it has materially aimed too high and moved too fast and has a chance now to show its strength by cutting back. Perhaps all concerned have not sufficiently kept the creative vision alive so that now the opportunity arises, happily, to catch up.

But this takes us beyond our present topic. No true and worthwhile success can be measured by externals, according to appearances, that goes without saying. Real success can be gauged only by those who in themselves truly succeed - even when they seem to fail. A measure of our success is that we learn from our failures. That kind of thinking is applied by creative teachers to their pupils in every detail of the day to day work and play.

*

14. Human and Anti-human

These are exciting times. The opportunity for coming to grips with the central issue of human survival is ours. We are politically at liberty to concern ourselves with it, we have the leisure time if we want it, we are economically supplied, scientifically supported, technologically equipped. We are in the possession of the mental and spiritual faculties required for a discerning look at what ails and besets us. Evolution, for what it's worth, has left us high and dry, meaning: culturally we enjoy the broadest possible overview while emotionally we are just possibly more miserable than ever – if we had the courage to become conscious of our misery.

These are exciting times. We may be a miserable lot, but we are uniquely blessed with a light in our midst that will allow us to come to terms with our misery and to draw strength out from underneath it. The nature of that strength is something worth crowing about; our self-sufficiency and individual independence is not. It may seem a pity that in a sense we have to confess our frailty before we can be substantially comforted, but in actual fact it's simply a law of human survival. When we experience the challenge we either fly in the face of it or make ready for a considerable investment. We either lie down under it and moan or we search for the sort of organic equipment we were all born with so as to deal with the matter in hand. Men and women are every day inspired by nature but it behoves them to fight the suspicion that this is not so. It's a glorious fight, well worth the effort. It may be fought on a million and one fronts.

Now human being is a precious commodity. Men and women will jealously guard it and introduce it judiciously to their children. They hire teachers to give them a hand, so that up-bringing and education can in fact go hand in hand. They don't all find it a simple matter to agree on a description of it, but the having of it seems more crucial than the dogma, so they agree on the riches of variety while meanwhile practicing hindsight and tolerance.

The funny thing about human being is that not only can it be gained but it can also be lost. And the European Court of Rights will not legislate. Nor will the International Union of Churches take responsibility for the supply. We ourselves, first one at a time, then three or four in concert, must see to that. And it can be an uphill struggle. This puzzles the mind. Why should it be such a tricky and downright onerous business when really what it amounts to is that we get what we have already? There must be forces that hinder us. There must be powers in whose interest it lies that we fail in our best efforts. No other explanation seems reasonable. Here we see mountains of food spoiling while there whole tribes of people starve. No one in his right mind prefers murder and mayhem to peace and love, and yet we are not always in our right minds.

We come to the conclusion that evil exists and that it does come into the world. We find it as difficult to come to an agreement about the description of evil as about the definition of human being, but it comes into the world all the same. It refuses to be put off by optimism or pessimism. It creeps in where we least notice, and subtle as you please.

The most subtle variety of all is what makes these times so exciting. When we look into the past we seem to notice how at one time it was man's freedom that was most at stake, at another time his virtue, or yet at another time the salvation of his soul, the development of his intelligence, the right to his dreams and mythologies, and so on. But what we detect today, by comparison, as the burning issue, is the human being's ability to be in actual fact a human being. Influences abound that would prevent that. It sounds paradoxical, as though one could at one and the same time be a human being and not a human being. You might say that we are born human beings and then gradually the human being is burnt out of us. You might also bear in mind that any given number of us can at any moment in time become more or less human. That may be a novel way to use the word 'human', but the times call for it. We have what it takes to detect those subtle anti-human influences today, those forces and energies that seem to exist precisely in order to deny the humanity in us, to empty us of it, to drain it out of our system – for a suitable reward of course. In the past, those who were willing to give up their freedom were granted an immunity to certain anxieties; of course it was kept from them that precisely in overcoming their anxiety lay freedom. Then, those who wanted to think for themselves were informed, by subtle influence, that orthodox systematic organizations were much better at it, and if one gave it up one was rewarded with a sort of herd security, an egotism en masse. Thirdly, there were the dreamers, with their original dreams, and each one could, if he chose, fashion them well for the comfort of many. But once again, since these fashioned dreams, like the thinking initiative and like the existential freedom, were conducive to humanity and investments of human being, they had to be made suspect, they had to be brought under the umbrella of the scientific sanction, because Science, the great Cyclops, tolerated no dreams but its own. So if you gave up your humanity-productive dream you were rewarded with a control over nature and the elements, which was supposed to reassure you, because now you could point at the quality, the value, the virtue - out there, and this was called evidence.

Today it seems that not so much some way to humanity is barred, such as personal freedom, original thought or imaginative dreaming, but humanity and human being itself. We are being undermined at the very foundation, the rot is setting in at the core. It's almost as if one last ditch attempt were being made, this time to corrode the essence of all being, so that anyone who says: "I find it difficult being a human being," will be laughed at, because, after all: "What are you in any case? You make far too much of yourself. Let go of these strange ambitions that would set you apart from the rest of creation. Believe only that a few years are yours and then back to sleep. You know fine well how it hurts to wake up. Pain is a set-back and we would relieve you of pain. We will pay you well if you stop pretending you are higher than the angels, even higher than the animals, than the elements. Your reward will be - unconsciousness even now, ahead of time. Sink below the elements and capture the heaven of the elect, of those who are perfectly happy not being. "To be or not to be" will not be a question for you any more, since you will quite simply mistake non-being for being, popularity for humanity, the rigour of death for the bliss of life. We will make that mistake utterly irreversible for you. You will never recognize it as an error, because you will lack the sensitivity for the comparison. Only give up this notion of yourself as in any way special, as in any sense attached to the universal centre of creation; that brings you nothing but stress, strife and struggle. Begin by listening to these soothing words of mine."

Something like an electric shock passes through a human being when he realizes suddenly what he is liable to lose. He clutches his liberty, his mind and his beliefs, but finds that nevertheless the wool is being pulled over his eyes and the rug out from under his feet. He gives himself a shake and begins to wonder about these voices whispering in his brain and about his indifference with regard to them hitherto. A totally new sphere of interest is claiming his attention and that is himself in person. Doubt is being cast on the very possibility of his effectiveness. His creature originality is being called into question. His awareness of his being as unlike that of all other beings is being trodden underfoot. The rational animal and the presumptuous god have had their day; what is left for him?

Beside him stands another like himself. He looks at him and experiences aversion. Right away perfectly legitimate justifications for that aversion crowd his brain and activate his limbs.

But from somewhere comes strength. He rejects those justifications and chooses love instead. He overcomes the aversion. Conversation ensues. Respect becomes possible, and a sense of propriety. Beyond the conversation extends a relationship. A mutual feeling of responsibility is entertained. An appetite for peace is satisfied. A third comes along, a stranger to both. She threatens their union. They form themselves into an exclusive society, only to find that their peace disintegrates, their respect for one another dissolves and mutual hatred sets in. Love grows beyond every one who makes use of it. Now they have

100

learned that. A conversation resumes, with the third, who seems less of a threat now. She brings new tidings: human nature has finally been set free. Only imagine, they had nearly excluded her! Never again will they hide behind a shadow of the world. They have discovered the joys of community and they refuse to account for it, for it grows with a spontaneity that amazingly takes care of itself.

Looking back, they ask what it was that nearly caused them to forfeit their humanity. They see others like themselves, at dire risk. If only they were aware! There are many who seem in a serious quandary as to which line to follow - the line of least resistance or the one that leads through thick and thin to the reward buried within themselves and willing to move into them.

Humanity is willing to move in and into us. It exists within us and desires to be discovered, while at the same time it exists without us, willing to move into us. We really have a marvellous choice here, as to which way we help ourselves. Both within and without, the true reality beckons. Either we lack it, and then surely we search for it, or else we have it, and then we know no greater ambition than to testify to it as effectively as possible. The passionate search and the compassionate testimony dovetail. Really there is very little room for any other kind of behaviour during such a crisis as besets us today. We either look for help or we seek to help, and ours is a common anxiety. The very nature of humanity is in that sense demonstrated.

The fashion of the times is that no human beings should come into existence and that those who exist should be anti-socialized as soon and as effectively as possible. Numerous societies are in fact set up, from some superficially laudable motive, but with the covert, and of course not self-confessed, ambition to cast suspicion on human being and to render humanity impotent. Naturally there cannot be any discussion with those who call the truth falsehood and falsehood the truth, for whom reality is delusion and delusion reality. At the crisis point only one course of action lies open, namely that we testify to the truth as we honestly perceive it, and that we do this with energy and compassion. Anti-human influence's surround us, but this need not disquieten us. Only if we neglect to discern them do we fall under their spell and the centre slips out of us - indiscernibly. What are the symptoms of chronic disintegration? Indifference and hysteria. As soon as we notice that these become fast in us, there is serious cause for concern. Hysteria is the sign that not our spirit or our soul, but we ourselves, as human beings, are at risk. And indifference, as an overall indefensible disposition, means exactly the same. Or we might call it a cynical indifference, where we feel we have just cause for it. Or our hysteria takes on all the trappings of a demand for justice. The chief anti-human impulse actually likes to cloak itself in these trappings of justice, so that we become persuaded of our need for it, of our inability to do without it.

So we do well to learn mercy. The tiniest merciful intention, not to mention a merciful act, re-establishes our humanity on a sound footing and clears our vision because it must discountenance every anti-human agency.

* * *

15. Instruction for Religion out of Everyday Experience

What a child needs to know and to feel can be developed out of his physical contacts with his contemporaries, if this knowledge and feeling is to give him some inward familiarity with his own human nature and human being. The organic connection between our various truthful inward experiences and the real world is what is largely missing nowadays. Children get older in a world they cannot respect and with inward dispositions that frighten them or leave them in the lurch. The creative teacher would take it upon himself to speak of the outward and of the inward to the child. This division should be acknowledged by the teacher, because the children by and large begin to experience this duality, and they are torn much as they are torn when their parents fight or divorce.

This experience of being torn is central to so many contemporary children's existence that we cannot do better than to set it at the beginning of our care for them. We ourselves, as mature adults, if we teach, must be entirely honest with ourselves and one another in our acknowledgment of this experience; it won't do if we pretend that we 'are good' and are therefore forced to deal with this topic on a hypothetical level. We ourselves must confess that we know what it means to be irreligious, to be torn between world and self, between personal relationship and individual need. No one can awaken religious being in children who is not himself persuaded of this most crucial need in our lives for being able to respond in a variety of ways to the twin experiences of burn-out and break-down.

Not that finally the universe exists in twos, or that the cosmos comes in hemispheres, or that human beings must have split personalities to survive! But if one is to return to, or to arrive at, the whole, the holy and the healed, one first of all has to acknowledge that one does in fact swing like a pendulum, temperamentally or psychically or even carnally, from an outside situation to an inside state and back again, and that these two experiences, albeit partial and fruitless in the main, do make up a great deal of what we call our life. And if we are able to heal, in ourselves and others, then we will be all the more ready to countenance that the wound exists.

So the teacher who hopes to educate in terms of religion brings to the attention of his pupils his contemporary external world on one side and his inward being and becoming on the other. These are two ways of facing for the child : inward and outward. There are the parents, the brothers, sisters and friends, the relations and acquaintances. These make the greatest external impression on children and they care most about how they fare with them. The teacher talks about them as outside and as outward experiences. He intentionally leaves out and away any consideration of how the pupils feel about these people, what they mean to him, why or why not he might seek their company. "Here are your parents," says the teacher. "They move in and out of the house. There are big houses and small houses. Archy, your house is a caravan. Parents take care of you; and those who take care of you, help you across the street, give you food, are like parents to you. You come to school with your friends. There are so many cars on the streets nowadays, and sometimes the air is thick with the smell of exhaust fumes. Some of your parents have to drive through that smog and they come home angry. They look for food, they want to complain to someone who will sympathize. The door opens, there stands your brother and a policeman holds him by the hand." And so on. The teacher takes pains to get to know intimately the external circumstances of every child. He asks questions, all pointed towards these, so that the pupil becomes conscious, while relating, of what he comes across every day 'out there'. The questions are put personally by the teacher to an individual pupil or to several, and the teacher knows that the principle virtue and effectiveness resides in the question, not in any answer. He knows what it means to a child to be earnestly addressed.

Then suddenly the teacher switches over and draws the pupil's attention to inward experience, such as for example the great amount of day-dreaming that goes on, and the images and fantasy that is a daily pastime of most children, though while they do it they don't know what they are doing. These inward experiences of feeling, imagination and fantasy are all dealt with on their own ground by the teacher and not related to anything external. "Who has ever been afraid?" he might ask, without mentioning any outside cause. "How do we feel when we're afraid? Here it feels tight, and here. And then we get a headache and sometimes very tired. Who has ever seen a very tired dream ship, with not a breath of wind for the sails?" So the fear is imagined, along with lassitude. "Your mind drifts off, you have nothing to think about; but who waits around the corner? Sam, who waits around your corner? What colour is that corner? You turn that corner and everything is silent, quiet, still. Imagine yourself sitting down on a rug when someone says to you: Don't sit there, stand up! - Don't stand there, you are in my way! - Do something, you look bored! - Don't look bored, look busy! – Oh dear, how do you feel after that? Don't tell me you are not going to become invisible. Who has an invisibility button? George, come up here in front and press your invisibility button."

According to the age, the usual experiences of the pupils, and above all as it occurs to him at the moment while intimately in contact with the pupils, the teacher measures out a terrain of inwardness, of inner awareness. Because he knows what he is doing, the children are not lost inwardly but a bridge is formed for them, by the teacher, to outward experience, in himself.

The teachers would school themselves in inward and outward inventiveness and awareness; they would get together to exercise their own fantasy and imagination; they would learn how to talk about their own emotion and feeling, right there on the spot, at length, at a moment's notice. One would begin very simply, always totally aware of the direction, of the strength on which one is drawing. They would perhaps begin with biography of one another, acknowledging how little they can repeat of the details of one another's existences, everything from birthday and telephone number to habits, hobbies and inhibitions. Biography and fantasy could then be mixed. Favourite phobias might be acted out, expectations described in practicable detail, limitations acknowledged.

What has all this to do with religion? Everything. When we cannot joyfully and meaningfully relate to our fellow man, we lack religion. When our inner life is a puzzle to us, or a torture chamber, we lack religion. When the world is a miserable rat race for us, devoid of adventure, mystery and real satisfaction - we lack religion. Religion is not something we have but something we do, under given circumstances. Every new impulse that comes into our lives or even into ourselves cannot but jar our system, upset our harmony, twist our sense of the past and present. If we are incapable of religion we never receive the gifts that come our way because we are too busy worrying about the changes they might cause in our status quo. Every misfortune is a messenger of glad tidings and without religion up our sleeves we are never done killing the messenger.

Those who would teach religion must know how to do religion, that goes without saying, otherwise the blind lead the blind. Consider only, for example, that the core of all religion is that you love your fellow man as though he were yourself. How can you love him if you don't take an interest in him, in his circumstances and in his personality and character? How can you love him if you run away from him as soon as he trusts you enough to reveal to you his shortcomings, or if you betray him as soon as he trusts you with his secret joys?

The man who is capable of religion has within him his god as creator, and creativity is his power for life. Religion gives shape to what would otherwise fall apart, such as marriage, friendship and companionship, and those growth relationships that we influence parentally and pedagogically. But first of all it holds together our spirit, soul and flesh. But not if we concentrate on these exclusive of one another. Religion is other-directed.

What I do for you reflects on me, what I do for myself may remain still-born.

What teachers of religion do for their pupils reflects on themselves a hundredfold, because they handle the very substance that nourishes life. They feed their pupils and show them how to get food for themselves. And celebrations announce themselves. When it's time to celebrate, those who have done religion cannot do otherwise. These words I have written amount to a celebration. What a dead thing is a celebration that is instituted as a means towards some end! Those who indulge in it can never believe it but must always try to make others do so.

The everyday experience of all children is manifold and various. We must find out what it is and then draw on it. There is outward and inward everyday experience, an endless amount in each category, and the teacher of religion learns to tap it. Outside there is the playground, the house and the car, clothes, toys and pets, food, pastimes, the garden, the field and the town, shopping, birthday parties; later on there are all the grown-ups who interact and are observed by the child, as they entertain one another, make political decisions, as they walk and run and sit still. The list of the things we can point at to which children have access is literally endless and every period of instruction may be centred on one or two. The interest that is encouraged is of course a very specific one, since one intends that the child should learn to distinguish between outward and inward experience so that eventually these two might be joined, or be revealed as joined, in a work and in works. Religion is precisely such a work. All true works testify to the wholeness and oneness of reality.

The inward experiences of pupils are just as numerous, but once again one must take the trouble of finding out what sort of inward experiences particular pupils have. Certainly children could not list them off, any more than most adults can. And when a child is familiar with inward pain he will be as reluctant to talk about it as an adult in that situation. But then we have no intention of talking about, to discuss it in any way, but we wish to refer to it and to let the child know that one can in fact safely refer to it. Inward pain is experienced by contemporary children in a way that makes them wish they were dead. There are all the experiences of disappointment, of a good mood or a bad mood, of high spirits of boredom.

There is the fever, the hyper-sensitivity, the shame. None should be touched on in reference to a supposed cause, because all too quickly do we all jump to conclusions when we contemplate causes. The dream, the daydream, the fantasy: all these from infancy to puberty, approached appropriately, in whatever way the pupils can manage and are willing to entertain. There is affection, hatred, distaste and liking. There is anger, lost temper and delirious happiness. All these have a certain individual feel to them to which the pupil can testify. He will describe how it felt - how it was - to be lost at the fair, to be full of mirth at the funeral, to sit back and imagine the teacher with an arrow through his forehead.

Every experience must be split into outward and inward.

* * *

16. Loving too much or too little

There is a way to love that can never be too much or too little, but alas, it eludes us. Then we can tell that it has eluded us because suddenly we suppose we love, or have loved, too much or too little.

Now while the very experience of loving too much or too little is a sign that the real love has eluded us, that same experience holds the key for regaining entry to real love - I mean the doing of it. And this is surely exceedingly good news! Because usually, if we fear we have loved too little, we step up our efforts and take all sorts of pains to make good the neglect, only to notice that the desired result is not forthcoming. We measure the 'more' we desire by the 'too little' we fear and the outcome is failure; our increased intentions and attentions are ill-starred. And the same thing happens on the other side of the divide, where we feel we have loved too much and so we suspect we should control our emotions and perhaps disabuse ourselves of certain illusions. We try to cut back, to cut our losses, and - cut into our own flesh. That is not too strong an expression, especially not for those who are by nature passionate and cannot give unless they give of themselves, and then preferably all of themselves. But here once again the supposed remedy we administer is not wisdom's child but an offspring of the fear, that we may have gone too far, that we may have exceeded our capacity - to love.

But there, precisely there, lies the information we need. We suppose that we have a capacity to love, to love more or less. The infatuated lover who demands: "How much do you love me?" is talking about something else. The jealous lover who demands: "You must love me and not these others!" is also talking about something else. What it is they mean does not so much concern us here as what we ourselves mean, which is otherwise.

We mean the way one human being loves another human being so as to do him or her good. This is what we call real love, in comparison to true love, which is hopefully on the way of becoming real love, and in comparison to all other sorts of so called love which are mere shadows and have more to do with possessiveness and self-indulgence than with anything else. Where greed comes into the picture the frame of awareness explodes and wickedness masquerades as love, while true love, instead of becoming real, is ashamed of us and must withdraw. Meanwhile we rage and storm, or languish and malinger, until we are once again burnt out or broken down.

Now we can approach real love either directly from true love, or indirectly, through the wise understanding of our experience of having loved too much or too little. There is good news for us here for when we have gone wrong, but equally it's good news to know we don't have to wait until we have gone wrong.

First there must of course be true love, this is indispensable. We cannot even make a mistake unless we first have a notion of the right way of it. And true love does in a sense happen to us. It must, for example, be true love that attaches teacher and pupils in a classroom. I mean the human natural affection that comes from the heart. Ah, but we know what else comes from the heart, not at all on the credit side of the balance sheet!

All the same, unless we experience a sincere and inward inclination towards another, where we would rather see him be well and do well than ill, we are not on the right track. We lose sight of this connection of love and the truth because so many things go wrong before this true love is realized, there are so many disappointments, frustrations, there is so much intense bitterness and ambition, that we throw out the baby with the bathwater. There are so many afflictions, once innocent true love raises its head only a little, that we lose hope and courage before we even get started. Indifference and cynicism, or at best the stoic retreat, are much less painful and, in the long run, from the point of view of survival, much safer.

So while most of us sadly have said a reluctant goodbye to true love, and therefore of course potentially to real love, so that the very word love scandalizes us and we will not have it, there are some few among us who refuse to cut themselves off from the source of life, even if this refusal should bring with it a variety of pain, such as guilt, shame, and the manifold derivatives of these.

These few - how fortunate for us if our teachers are among them! No one can teach unless he lives, and no one can live unless he loves - and no one can love unless his love is at first true.

If I truly love someone and that someone insults me I experience sharp pain and, lo and behold, my true love turns to real hatred! I can say quite correctly that I truly loved, but alas, now I hate, and this hatred justifies itself in leaps and bounds. I am willing to kill the one I loved.

But, to be perfectly honest, the true love happened to me, and I did nothing to support it. To put it more succinctly, I happened to love, but I did not love; I did not do so. Came the affliction of the insult, and where was my love? Turned to hatred. And life? Turned to death. I will even take pleasure in this vengefulness that comes over me, as I feel licensed to punish the one who did not return my love – my love? - but instead insulted me.

It's not my love at all until I have realized it. Quickly, as soon as I experience this human natural affection from the heart, let me not just feel it and hug it to myself but let me do it and act it out. True love lends itself most appropriately to creation. It wants to do good, first inwardly then outwardly. It desires to countenance the light of day and not be smothered in darkness. And, above and beyond all, it delights in withstanding affliction, in overcoming hardship, in the intelligent suffering of pain. Weakness means that love is at that moment teaching us completion. Flagging energy means that real love is at that moment at work on our behalf. Unless we know this, we fear these. But if we find ourselves fearing these, why not draw on this knowledge to overcome the fear and learn real love, again and again?

*

Real love eludes us, then, because we try to make do with true love, which has happened to us, like a sunny spring day, and instead of hoeing and sowing we only enjoy the weather. We neglect to make a real distinction between our passions, with their sense of business and reward, their warm, close feelings, their emotions of being indispensable and invulnerable, and passion, which is basically our willingness to suffer and undergo. Passion is peaceful and always at rest. What we really do passionately does not weary us or tire us out, but neither does it give us any great sense of self-importance, so that if someone were to accuse us of not pulling our weight we would experience no burning need to justify ourselves but we would simply forgive the mistake.

So a great weakness overcomes us and we are not at all any more able to be productive, to function as a matter of fact. We compare our present weakness to the memory of our strength - and we despair. We push all the usual buttons but nothing happens. Indeed we experience a frightening sense of worthlessness. Whatever has happened to us?

We have arrived at the crisis between productivity and creativity. Very few seem to know about this critical point, about this way station on the path of growth.

Productively we do our best, with all our available material resources and we operate to the full extent of our development as human beings right now. Then comes the time when we have so to speak proved ourselves, and now we are to go beyond doing our best. We are to do good. We are to progress from productivity to creativity. What a pity if we mistake this stage of our growth! We have crawled very successfully, now we are to learn how to walk. So crawling is made difficult for us. But we refuse to walk. Ah well, if we insist. Back we go to crawling. Perhaps we were the smoothest crawlers on our patch and are reluctant to relinquish our status, little realizing that the smallest among us in reality is greater than the greatest by nature.

There is a productive love, and then there is a creative love. We know that the time is ripe for the latter when the former runs out. Lack of energy, failing strength, these are the signs; and a mounting anxiety about that 'black hole' in the future, because we cannot predict along customary lines of experience.

The transition from the one love to the other can go smoothly. We can interpret the signs correctly, at once, and once we have done it a few times we get better at it. We feel that our best efforts are stymied: there comes that tell-tale panic over the horizon - and creativity takes over. By creativity we don't mean picture drawing, basket weaving or piano playing, but an inward allowance made for the fact that love is greater than any of our understanding, and this combined with a glad willingness to be changed to the good by that love, even as we testify to it in some work, and our work might be speech or silence. The productive lover is blissfully unaware of the fact that he himself is being loved at that very moment, and what he produces, if he does his work well, liberates and cleanses. Perhaps he will never be challenged by that great responsibility implied by creativity and brought home to some by the influence on them of creative love. In that case he will not experience the productivity crisis, where things as they are seem to come to an end; where he at one and the same time wishes to shake off a great weight and yet panics at the thought of the lack of that gravity. He will continue to serve, and his service is called his vocation, and within the confines of that vocation he functions honourably, and with due respect and reverence for those who are chosen to love creatively. He knows who they are and he honours them in thought and in deed, for he benefits from their work.

But those who experience the challenge of creative love can take it for granted that they have what it takes to meet that challenge. This love does not rise in those who have not the capacity for acknowledging it.

A typical initial, automatic-reaction to this love-experience is a fear that one does too much or too little - that one has loved, or loves, too much or too little. We must give more of ourselves! No, we are over-committed, over-engaged, we need a total release, a complete change. But then we will lose touch, lose ground, so really we cannot afford to make a break - and so on. We are tantalized by illusions and we torture ourselves.

Be still and know that all is well. Let yourself be shaped, in readiness for a task you cannot yet fathom but you will grow into it. Make contact with the body of your panic, and though you feel nothing, know that this love brings you all. Just then it goes on, while you are still and feel nothing. Let your main work be trust. You are being sought out for a special contribution to the world of reality, to your fellow human beings.

But if you insist now on the force of your past ways, on the energy of yesterday, on last year's satisfaction, you effectively say no to your new being; you reject your creator. From your creator comes the creative love that would change you into one who loves creatively. Within you the urge to make great things happen does battle with the desire to bring good things about. The wish to have nothing but time on your hands competes with the ambition to be absolutely independent. But this is only the other side of that apprehension that you love too little or too much. It amounts to the same.

Creative love can never be too little or too much because what we offer to others is first and foremost their freedom. This freedom can only be offered, and therefore we have to first create it in ourselves. However, every encounter with another initially inhibits our freedom, so our creative love of that other one begins each time again with a recreation of that freedom in ourselves, so that we can offer it, for the other to accept. If he refuses, we cannot coerce him to be free.

A creative teacher's chief ambition is to always and again recreate freedom in himself, which is not principally a liberation from his own pain, such as interests the artist, but a glad acceptance of the unfortunate bondage of others, unwittingly transferred to him. The central pedagogic aim is redemptive.

* * *

17. Modern to Contemporary

Modernity has been with us for nearly two-thousand years and today we have the option to see that fact in perspective. We are able to describe as modern, for instance, any attempt to know space and time as separate from each other. Modern man wants to isolate time so that he can predict it. He wants to know 'the time'. And to the extent that we ourselves are still modern we are bound to say: "And why should he not? If he does not know the time, how can he be ready?"

We in turn are bound to ask: "Ready for what?" We can see how modern man wants to be ready for the event pending, for the future event, which exists in the future in the first place because of how he has behaved towards time. His penchant for scientific prediction in a thousand

and one directions is a symptom of his unwillingness to leave time in itself alone. Because he neglects to search in himself for the rhythm of his existence he becomes tactless in the face of the event. This tactlessness is his modern shortcoming.

Due to this shortcoming modern man finds himself literally with space on his hands. Since he has forced time out of all real perspective, space has become something like a commodity for him, and while on one hand he can never quite get enough, on the other hand it causes in him an unholy panic. The very same impulse of 'space on the loose', as we might call it, drives one man into a monastic cell and turns the other into an imperialist. Because space seems suddenly a boundless commodity, divorced from time, one can never get enough of it and one is never 'at peace with it, truly sheltered, in one's modernity.

When we speak of the rhythm of our existence we touch on the very thing that modern man avoids as he 'wants to know the time' instead. What is it that is so much more attractive about 'knowing the time'? What is it about this rhythm that frightens us?

We have within us something like an organic clock. We have moved, over the past twenty centuries, so far away from any familiarity with this clock that the suggestion of it now strikes us perhaps as absurd, perhaps as somehow inspired. However, something else has to be considered before we can be squarely in the picture. Not until nearly twenty centuries ago did we come into the possession of this organic clock. So we have to define modern man from two directions. He is modern because he came into the possession of this clock and - because he ignored it and chose to know the time instead. He should have identified his contemporary rhythm. Since he did not do what he should have done he is guilty. He feels that guilt and tries his best to cope with it, but' alas! While he continues to be modern, wanting to know the time and ill at ease in divorced space, the guilt cannot diminish; it will only change its face. Yesterday it was a moral guilt. Today it is an existential guilt. Tomorrow it will be economic. Economic guilt is just these days beginning to be felt. The newspapers, the journals, the mass media are full of it, though it has not yet risen into consciousness to the point where drastic measures will have to be taken to rule out the presumed cause of it.

A man becomes contemporary as soon as he begins intentionally to sense his inward chronology. "Now this is happening to me," he says, "and now this. It seems I am being moved to identify my most secret motivations." A careful perusal of that last sentence, as worded by our friend, lets us in on his secret. He is being moved to know his motivations. A profound sense of affliction passes momentarily before his eyes and then he experiences loss. He experiences what modern man should have experienced but he chose to know the time, never could, and then knew guilt instead. He still goes on knowing guilt, but hopes to stop that as soon as he finally has correctly identified the time.

The loss a contemporary man experiences is the loss of his chronic being. The way he was, so tied into the seasons that he knew no better, this was his chronic being. Really he had no choice over the coming and going of his thoughts and feelings, this ancient man, and he longed for a distinct sort of freedom. He knew in himself that eventually this freedom would be on the cards and he longed for 'the day of the Lord', or for some such event, when his faculties and functions should not any more be indiscriminately harnessed to the elements in confusion. Heaven seemed righteous but needed to be confirmed. The earth seemed fruitful but there was no guarantee. Ancient man began to search within himself and recognized upon a sudden the distinct possibility of a release 'one day'. A great deal depended on how he behaved. But the liberation had to come in its own sweet time. All one could do was be as prepared as possible.

Then the liberation took place, hurray, and those who were ready and prepared took note of that amazing sense of loss, and they said to one another: "We must concentrate on the liberation and totally ignore that sense of loss, for it argues against everything we expected and were led to expect. No, let us celebrate at all cost a sense of fulfilment, for that is what we ought to experience, considering the fact of our liberation. Let us go so far as to pretend to such a sense of fulfilment, artistically if you like. Perhaps we should even intimidate those who gainsay this pretence because do they not belie the liberation? The liberation is a fact, we must hold to that, and we must coerce others, and shame one another, into a pretended sense of fulfilment, even as one would expect upon total liberation. He who in future mentions that sense of loss - may he be accurst! He shall be cast from the fold of those who are in fact liberated and are willing to pretend that they feel like it, as they expected they would.

The modern age had begun. Can we not feel the wind whistling between the chinks? The great Pretender, the spirit of pretence, had entered upon the stage, chock-a-block with metaphysical artistry.

What a tremendous bulwark modern man has erected to protect the fact of his liberation from his ancient chronic being against that sense of loss that 'should simply not have been the case'! He begins now, today, to encamp within a fortress of domestic principles in order to be safe from domestic, economic, guilt.

But facts are not truth. The fact of ancient man's liberation is indubitable, though in the flesh of modern man it looks less like a liberation and more like an excommunication. Never mind. Perhaps appearances deceive.

The truth of ancient man's liberation is yet to be discovered on a large scale. A few contemporary men have found it immensely difficult to delude themselves over that peculiar sense of loss, and since the hierarchy of modern factual man just seemed to be looking the other way for a moment, perhaps being tired or preoccupied by a new fact, these contemporary men took the time to examine what lay behind that sense of loss, and why did the pain become so much more intense as soon as one tried to ignore it? It seemed to suffice to simply assume the fact of the liberation in order to feel quite at liberty to examine this peculiar sense of loss; to examine it - and to examine the truth of it.

The truth of that sense of loss turns out, upon examination, to be a singularly contemporary experience. While one suffers that experience one is not swept away into other regions of thought and feeling, beyond the here and now, supernaturally speaking, but one remains clear eyed and with one's integrity in tact. It seems, therefore, a worthwhile undertaking. Above all, no more pretending is necessary. What a relief! So what if there is not a sense of fulfilment but a sense of loss, as long as the experience of it is truthful. And strangely enough, let it be noted, upon patiently suffering that sense of loss for a time it definitely seems to become less painful, less of a shameful and harrowing experience. Patience seems to be doing its work. Besides, it still seems a fact that an unpleasant truth beats a gratifying pretension, so this contemporary person decides, as he carves out his bit of meaningful reality for himself, carving, so to speak, against the grain.

Meanwhile his modern compatriots will certainly be regarding him collectively and through narrowed eyelids. Modern man clings to his dispossessed facts with a much more collective warmth when the time has come to excommunicate a transgressor. Remember the definition of the transgressor: anyone who puts at risk the pretend sense of perfection and progress on the side of liberty as a fact by giving credence to that sense of loss - even though that very sense of loss, let's face it, testifies to a real victory over the ancient chronic being. That sense of loss has nothing to do with intellectual assent or with a belief-system one has to swallow only to suffer ever after from indigestion, but it implies an actual physical and organic connection with that which has, after all, already replaced the chronic being, namely free, or human being.

We are, therefore, not on ideal, but on real ground if we do something that might be described as seeing that existential sense of loss through. Should we simply compare it to the pain after the operation? There is a better comparison. I am thinking of what his disciples went through after Jesus of Nazareth, their master and friend, had been taken from them. What they had been led to expect had, to them, not at all looked like that. From within their chronic being they had naturally construed the future facts in a different light. Now suddenly, although they had their freedom, they were all the same overwhelmed by a sense of loss. Some of them threw in the towel and decided to go back to their chronic being, but oh horror! they stared into an abyss. Others drew up a plan of action based on past expectations. Facts were fats and he who gave in to despair was a renegade. A faith was defined and then vigorously defended against other, infidel faiths, which defence allegedly strengthened it. A creed was constructed and finely honed, through centuries of intellectual patristic labour and with the aid of several high-power, think-tank type committee meetings, so that anyone who repeated it frequently enough could be sure to find himself on the right side, among the righteous.

And a few others, the contemporaries, said: "Let's wait, let's be still and see what happens. He did mention something about coming back, though we could never quite fathom the wording, probably because our chronic. expectations clouded the picture. We can see those clouds now and they hang over us like a curtain of despair. But let them hang for the time being. Did he not repeat something about appearing on the clouds? Let's not tear the curtain down, let's patiently wait until it opens of its own accord, because then we can be sure that the play of human reality and of real humanity is ready to begin.

Lo and behold! - as soon as they had made that quiet inward contribution to the creative plan, the curtain did open - for them. Always and again it can only open for contemporary men, that curtain. The moderns, of whatever century, storm the stage in their righteous certainty based on fact and intellectual justification and they tear the curtain down and - put on their own play. It's a modern drama, half tragic and half comic and the history of the last two millennia is the record, the script.

For contemporary men, these last two millennia do not really exist. They exist, but as a fiction, a myth. When the curtain opens for contemporary men, women and children, the metaphor breaks down and they find themselves in the sensible possession of genuine human being and eternal life. Our joy is complete now, just as previously our sense of loss was thorough and all-pervasive. But we did not let that throw us.

Modern man must return to that real sense of loss. He has to let go of all those artistic fictions with which he tries to anaesthetize his sense of loss, politically, psychologically, theologically, etc., and if it helps him to call to mind that what he has lost is in fact what he has always wanted to be rid of, then why should he not do that? Contemporary men and women – his own contemporaries! – cannot even begin to help him until he stops trying to beat the time, madly.

* * *

18. On the difference between religion and Religion, with reference to education

An important, a downright crucial thing to realize, if we want to make a useful impact on our human environment, is that Religion does not necessarily have anything to do with religion. It's possible to be a good Christian and an existential nonentity at one and the same time. When I speak to those who would convert me, on my doorstep, to their particular creed, which is like an agenda of pictorial representations to which they hold fast, I am always and permanently at a loss for human contact. Holding fast to a creed is not only unhuman, it dehumanizes. I ask these people into the house, bring them tea, try to make intimate contact with them - to no avail. I have often tried it. I have not yet succeeded. Not on the spot, in any case.

Not that only the evangelical door to door salespersons of Religion hold fast to a creed. The Orthodox Established Church, of whatever kidney, holds to a creed even faster, of course, often with proud condescension or aloofness, in comparison to the congenial seductiveness of the evangelist. And there is the lay preacher, who usually requires no more than three or four 'fastenings' for his loud and insistent repetition of his creed.

But it should really not be necessary to point to any of this in detail. Perhaps it would make more sense if we admitted that religion is possible even within the context of a Religion; at least the beginnings of it. What frequently happens is that someone finally has to cast off the Religion so that he can develop his religion.

We have mentioned elsewhere that religion is something to do. In comparison to that, Religion is something to pretend. By 'pretend' I mean everything from a serious or a frivolous playacting to a stress laid on what we would emphatically like to be the case while it is all the while not the case.

Needless to say, I am not concerned here over the true state of affairs in the breast of John Miller, Christian. What any given historical person calls himself is not always in line with what he really is. We have all met self-declared atheists who were more sincere in their humanity than self-declared lovers of God, and vice versa. While we develop and mature, we fight our way through a welter of contradictions, we go through formative 'phases', we reject today what we upheld yesterday – this comes along with being alive and not dead. All I have in mind to do here is to sort some of the materials that we make use of as we try to deepen and widen our knowledge and experience.

So, to restate our premises, Religion does not necessarily have anything to do with religion. But then neither does religion necessarily have anything to do with Religion.

For simplicity's sake, I prefer the ancient definition of religion as love of god and fellow man, and then the update of it as: love of god and fellow man not on that hill or in this building but in reality.

It's this business of 'in reality' that separates the men from the boys, and the doing from the pretending. I don't mean to imply, by the way, that all pretending is pretence and pretentiousness. Some pretending is devout, sincere, zealous, even ecstatic. But it's still pretending. And the truth of that matter is that the smallest one in reality is greater than the greatest pretender.

It helps us, surely, to keep in mind, that religion is small, that it knows of "these little ones", that it doesn't advertise in the market place, through a megaphone, but

it delights in secret conversation with the creator and up-
holder of all that lives. The sun always shines where religion is being done, which is mostly within and among
ourselves, but where Religion goes on, you are liable to
have Crusades, crucifixions, book-burnings, harangues,
excommunications, not to mention the great buckets full
of sweetness-and-light sentimentality, the nature reverence, the angel worship, the spiritualism and transcen-
dental metaphysics that crop up everywhere as mere reactions to these. The hard Religions and the soft Religions both aggravate each other and feed off each other.
Those who have had it hard for a while want to have it
soft now, and the other way around. But this is older than
the struggle between Amenhotep the third and fourth.

*

The pretending that goes on as Religion is not 'just
pretending'. It's usually a very serious business. We can
make ourselves believe whatever we like, but that still
doesn't mean that we have it in our bones. Through pretending we cannot realize a thing. We can only be more
or less adamant about what we adhere to, subscribe to or
proscribe. All the same, every Religion has this supposition embedded in its fabric somewhere, that if we just
pretend hard enough or soft enough we will eventually -
what? Come through? Arrive? Be good and true and
beautiful? But it cannot happen like that. Which is why
one Religion displaces another, and why there are always
so many, and why each is the 'only true one' to its adher-
ents. Of course there are tolerant Religions too, but their
way is then to admit (or insist) that there are many ways
of pretending and no one has the right to tell anyone else
how to pretend.

127

The unique thing about religion is that it combines what we learn with what exists in ourselves already. The reason we are able to do religion, so that we have neither cause nor need to pretend, is that we can count on our human nature, on what we were born with. We bring the ability and aptitude to do religion into the world with us. Then we need to be raised and educated in such a way that aptitude and ability become deed and then act. No amount or type of exposure to Religion or to Religions can help us in that. On the contrary. The more it's brought home to us that pretending, however sensible and intelligent, is worthwhile, important and good, the further are we estranged from our human naturally instinct religion. which then atrophies.

Now the way to prevent this atrophy from happening can be seen as a twofold one. There is religious education and there is instruction in religion.

First we need to acknowledge that all worthwhile education is religious. How could it be worthwhile if it neglected to take into account every child's inborn longing to link up his individuality with his environment, self with world! How could it be a useful up-bringing if it did not aim for personal communion in every which way?

So when we say education and up-bringing, we automatically say religion too, because we know how human beings come into the world and how human nature must be raised to awareness. Those who hear the word 'education' and think only of reading, writing and arithmetic, pointing towards computer technology, art criticism and a successful law practice, are just not thinking right or smart. So we distinguish between standard and creative education. We can equally speak of standard and creative religion, where Religion is standard.

Then we can recognize that the religion readily disappears out of education and so we can actually instruct religion. We can place special emphasis on it, in recognition of the fact that special emphasis is in fact being placed almost everywhere on removing religion out of life and out of education, most successfully in our times by way of the most sophisticated mass media. So instruction of religion would be an educational corrective and preventative in face of the mass media culture. We cannot even properly estimate the pernicious influence of this cult of the mass media until we undertake such a corrective. Not until then do we know what we're up against.

And it would make sense to take care that the instruction of religion has nothing to do with Religion or with Religions. If it did, that would be self-defeating. We can overlook all the Religions of the world today, and certainly we may find them interesting as phenomena, from a variety of viewpoints, anthropological, historical, mythological and so on. We could even include them as curricular subject-matter during the course of creative education, so that Religion would stand beside Geology, Chemistry, Cybernetics, Spelling, etc. as something to talk about while pupils are being educated. But Religion on the curriculum would make children no more mindful of their ability to love god and those around them in reality than Chemistry on the curriculum makes them more chemical.

Every teacher of creative education is of course free, and should wish to be free, to choose his own means and devices for refreshing, reconstituting and recreating himself. What counts is that he does it, not how he does it. I myself, for example, rely heavily on the feed-back I get from my own creative activity. Creativity works outward and inward at the same time. I also depend on some good habits that were instilled in me during my own upbringing. For behaviour I find most useful the ethics suggested by Jesus of Nazareth, and I consider him as the Christ or Messiah at the centre of what I call reality. Now I certainly would not argue with anyone about this, nor would I wish to persuade anyone to adopt my own favourite methods for nourishing my human being. However, when I meet someone who is in need of such nourishment, I find I can be most effective by limiting myself to ordinary, everyday language and behaviour while inwardly, and so to speak in secret, doing the necessary. I do it in secret, inwardly, not because I want no one to know that I do it, but because that is where it works best. The one I call god allows me to co-operate with him most congenially in secret. I can do what I do within the confines of my own human being contemporary with whatever else I do. Better than that, unless I do this religion, within, I cannot succeed in anything outward. I can make a big noise and draw attention to myself, but not have lasting good effect. And the other, related thing worth mentioning is of course that any lasting good effect is not necessarily traced back to me by anyone But I have the benefit of having created it all the same.

*

So there is Religion as a creed, as an ideology and a belief system, and there is religion as a way of inwardly doing good that has permanent outward consequences. People do not necessarily opt for the one or for the other. There are those who maintain that Religion is better than no religion at all, but I wonder. It would seem to me that Religion is a hindrance to religion, in that we cannot pretend to be human beings and be human beings at the same time. It stands to reason that the pretending we do involves self-delusion first, and then delusion of others. And self-delusion is a tenacious wickedness on one hand, but also a terrible misfortune. Those who have once tasted the magic of self-delusion, especially after a period of dryness, frustration and disappointment, are often eager to repeat the experience, to hedge it round with stimulus and exclusivity and to underpin it with strenuous justification.

Now religion, in comparison, is work. It involves sober self-examination, moral hygiene, chastity, acquired good habits such as waiting and suffering in cheerfulness, and constant application, experimentation and learning. It involves the willingness to stand alone and to shun the crowd. It can never be popular. It presents every single man and woman with individual challenge and testing. The result is real life right here and now. True religion is not a quick solution to anything but part and parcel of the way we exist, meaningfully, restfully and peacefully, gratefully and joyfully. Adults these days are being presented with recipes for instant liberation, and often this liberation takes the form of a cultivated absence of pain with nothing to show for it. It would seem rather crucial to teach children what is required to withstand this search for mere liberation so that they might shoulder their individual burden for the sake of actual freedom. Religion is sometimes desired as mere liberation, and then a Religion comes in handy and religion is not considered. The turning point is attitude towards misery, pain and death, and this hinges on an understanding of the reason for our being here, which is not to be happy or miserable, but to live. And children carry this perception within them, but it does become buried under wickedness, falsehood and ugliness. The instruction of religion addresses this problem directly and emphatically. Education in general must address it indirectly, while the pupil, so to speak, is looking elsewhere. The morality of our children should not be based on precepts of Religion but it should grow organically out of constant religion.

* * *

19. Psyche and Soul

We do well not to use these two words interchangeably. Our soul is one thing, and with right do we call it ours, because we are either in the possession of it or else it makes no difference to us, so that, in the course of meaningful language, it makes no sense whatsoever to speak of 'the' soul. There is my soul, if I have one, and there is yours, if you have one. What that is, and what it amounts to, when we do have it, we shall look at in a moment.

First we need to acknowledge that it happens that we are not in the possession of our soul. This either happens at times, or it goes on for long periods of time. It is even possible that we permanently lose our soul.

At such times as when we are without our soul we are psychic. What it means, to be psychic, and what can only be described as being 'under the influence' of a psyche, or as 'being possessed' by a psyche, can only be understood from the point of vantage of a working soul. Only a person with such a soul can help someone who is possessed by psyche. The one who is possessed in this way does not always know it, nor does he always know that he needs help. But he is, and he does.

Psychology can therefore be practiced only from the level of a possessed or owned soul, while depth-psychology presupposes a soul on a high level. Depth and height have equal rights to qualification here.

The loftier soul might rescue the more depressed psyche - myth works successfully within those boundaries..

To be psychic, to be under the influence of psyche, means first and foremost to be in a state of insufficiency. Complex longings are unsatisfied. Perplexing depressions remain unresolved. There is a harrowing back and forth between self-hatred and self-congratulation, between fear and adoration of others and the world. Mood swings draw on seemingly unlimited resources of energy or a plague of indifference draws the pitiable individual into one illness after the other. The affective life is stimulated apparently for no other reason than that the carrier of it should experience betrayal. Spiritually not much is managed beyond a sporadic enthusiasm and degrees of visionary depletion.

A study of the psyche - and we can speak meaningfully of 'the' psyche - from the point of vantage of our operational soul is either historical and in time or pointless.

Such a study limits itself intentionally to a particular time, and knows its own setting, or else veers off into chaos, to seduce and to mislead. The comments in the previous paragraph in reference to the psyche apply specifically, therefore, to what we today experience when possessed by psyche. It would be uninformed and unwise of us to refer to the psyche as though it might exist independently from individuals of one sort or another. It possesses you, or me, or someone else, otherwise there is no such thing. Its most frequent occurrences nowadays can be charitably talked about.

There is such a thing as an explanation, or reason, for the occurrence of psyche. Any psychic influence, or affect, is not merely accidental but significant. A psychic affect that reaches into our depth is profoundly significant. A coldly rational attitude would dismiss, even reject, the psyche, or instances of psyche. This is not well done. On the other hand, a boldly irrational involvement would stimulate, intensify, even sublimate it, and this is ill done.

Either we participate, detrimentally, in some form of rejection or sublimation of the psyche, or else we act on behalf of the potential soul, aware of the significance of the psychic state. There is no middle ground.

And what is the significance, in general, of psyche? That a soul is to be regained. In particular, 'a' psyche is the shadow cast by a distressed soul, and we can begin to move towards the healed, or whole soul by responsibly taking account of this shadow. This would seem to be a suitably contemporary description.

Certainly we do well to keep our soul, and in our patience we possess it, so by all means be patient and avoid impatience. (What! Nowadays? Precisely.) However, once you have lost your soul, it still exists, so do not despair. Let us together look at this thing you have instead, this psyche. It really helps if we do this together, because you on your own are tending to despair, I can tell. And even this despair is a psychic phenomenon. I shall think my own thoughts about it now, about this phenomenon, and I will say to you only the chosen words. Believe me, your psychic state has influenced, has affected me, and this is fine by me, for I know two things: one, I cannot help you back to your soul unless I have first-hand physical knowledge of your significant psyche, and two: I will gain in my own soul by helping you back to yours.

Your psyche, which the rationalist in me would fearfully reject and which the irrationalist in me would ambitiously manipulate - the human being in me would embrace lovingly. How dreadfully difficult for me to side with the human being in me! The agony and he ecstasy of the irrationalist seem so much more attractive. The might and the arrogant detachment of the rationalist are so much more appealing. Back and forth I stray between these two, really under the influence of the same psyche that possesses you, getting to know it in detail after a measure and - after the flesh. For the time being we are both in the same boat, which leaks, while the storm builds. I must find my way through to the human being in me, and I will succeed as soon as my perception of the affective psyche vis-à-vis my owned soul and your potential soul gains significant ground.

The effective therapeutic handling of psychic, and especially of depth-psychic, states proceeds in terms of suffering. True psychotherapy is a case of effective suffering for another. If you wish to heal me of my psyche, you must take my soulless state upon yourself, because only then will the healing word occur to you. It will not occur to you in reference to some recipe or method that leaves you separate and detached from me, nor will it occur to you if you too merely end up in pain and so we are both in pain and, drastically put, either die or kill each other.

If you would suffer on behalf of me in my psychic, soulless state, and if you would gain the due reward, it will not do for you to fall in with my pain or to argue and explain my pain away but you must suffer it. What does that mean? How can you do that?

A word about my soul now, when I do possess it. It operates as my soul, this is important to keep in mind, and there are such works which stem directly from my soul. But my soul occurs also on one hand as my body and on the other hand as my mind. Statically perceived, my mind and my body are face and obverse of my soul. Dynamically, there are the products of my mind, the fruits of my body and the works of my soul. My mind implies my soul and my body involves it. My body is the sum-total of all my available sense plus emotion, feeling and passion. My mind means thought, meditation and contemplation plus reflection. What a rich feast is my soul! What abundance of action and variety of behaviour!

How shall I choose now: soul or psyche?

But if I would possess my soul and its physicality in all its real concreteness, as a growing and mature human being, I cannot afford to rest on my laurels but I must with exceeding gladness suffer the pain of your psyche. Both the highest delirium and the lowest dejection of 'your' psyche cannot but cause me pain. Everything between these two extremes - cannot but cause me pain. How beneficial for both of us if I learn how to suffer!

Analysis can serve me. I need to examine how I shrink time and again from the single crucial act in the presence of your psychic state. But I must keep in mind that while no two souls are one and the same, all psychic states and all psyches are the same, are one and the same, inasmuch as they signal a greater power of soul. This is what chiefly should interest us about any psychic state or about any individual human being under psychic influence. There is no real cause to delve in dreams, to haruspicate, to plumb the so-called sub-conscious. What could we possibly gain there? Superstitions and idols.

Every psychic state, if we but knew it, heralds a greater power of soul. My soul casts a shadow because I have not yet faced up to an increase of light . Why would you argue with this shadow? Help me face up to the light, so that we both might see more clearly what appears in the new light.

Artists as such are never sufficiently consequent in relation to psychic phenomena. What we call artistry, in comparison to the art of the art worker, remains always to some extent, by connivance or choice, under the influence of the psyche, for money or fame. He stops being an artist and becomes an art worker as soon as he opts for concrete soul and for the intelligent and compassionate suffering of psychic states on behalf of his fellow human being.

But how can I suffer on your behalf what I sense you are going through in terms of psyche? Every fibre in me shrinks from the pain. This pain tends to dictate my action and regulate my behaviour. Psyche is pain for the one who knows it as psyche, though the one who is possessed by it, sickened, made ill, maddened – may actually experience this as a pleasure. There is an addiction to psyche, just as there is something like an anti-addiction to the rationalist rejection of psyche and the irrationalist indulgence in psyche. The addiction and the anti-addiction are liable to feed on each other. What about the one, now, who would increase the power of his soul; is he fighting a losing battle? How can we suffer such a pain that is tied up even with the principle of pleasure? Surely this task is impossible. The performance of it will have to be shown to me. If someone were pointed out to me who demonstrated such implicit trust in eternal human souls that he suffered even their collective psyche as it grew in proportion to his closeness to them, then I might myself come up with such trust, for I would be able to imitate and I would take courage from the fact that it had been done. If such a one existed now, or had existed in the past, or both, why, then my task should be easier, since I would only have to learn to lean on him, especially when the pain gets worst and suffering least likely, as fear paralyses affection and hatred destroys the world.

But where should such a one have lived? And under what circumstances? Would the popular mind not have falsified his memory and made a sham of his achievements? Would his tale not be told in terms so entirely psychic that a veritable psychology of him would have to be invented so as to rid these times of the false light obscuring the new light?

Best forget 'these times' and concentrate on our own time. Perhaps we have overlooked something - or someone. If we can see the thing that is required, how came we into the possession of that eyesight? Therein resides a mystery. Perhaps if we extend our trust on trust, not only where we feel on evidence that it is deserved – ?

The final relinquishment of the psychic ego can be terrifying. A few have managed it. We do well to look to them for guidance. They have suffered it through, with who knows whose help, so that their psychic ego has been replaced by themselves in the realm of a whole soul.

⅄ ⅄ ⅄

20. Religion as art

Demonstrate for someone that you know who your god is. Your god is perhaps not the same as mine, but considering that religion has to do with god, you might as well show me what yours amounts to. What is your religion? This may be like saying: who or what is your god? If your god is money, then you will deal with money religiously. You will be persuaded that money is the link between yourself and happiness, between yourself and joy, between yourself and virtue. If your god is popularity, prestige and fame, then those particular concepts will seem to fill you with awe and veneration.

So when we suggest that religion has to do with god, we have to add: What god. What is in a person's mind that he associates with god? Or what does he mean by good? What, for him, is the greatest good? It may be advancement in society, professional expertise, leisure and pleasure, health and welfare. All these things may mean to him what is good, and that which removes them or militates against them is bad.

Now the desire to demonstrate to others what we mean by 'good' is something of an exceptional urge. We do not so much want to be good to them, or even to do them good, but we simply want to show them what it is that we value so highly that nothing seems greater to us. We want to praise our god in front of others. We want to celebrate our relationship or connection with that greatest good out in the open where others can see and perhaps join us.

It's a curious pastime, but most of us participate in it to some extent, perhaps without being entirely conscious of it. People get together and do something they call 'having a party'. Their holy trinity may be leisure, ease and conviviality. Those who join them must worship at that shrine. Someone whose god is energy, craft and cunning will very likely not show up there. His party is political. Probably neither party would agree that they worship a good, or that they celebrate what they consider to be good, but that is what they do all the same. If they go to a church on Sundays, they bring their god with them and sacrifice to him on an altar. The priest says 'god', but the one man hears leisure, ease and conviviality, while the other man hears energy, craft and cunning. Whatever refuses to match these 'goods' they allow to pass by.

So one reason for celebrating the good we decide on is to lend it longevity and, if possible, permanence. It lies in the nature of a celebration that we take special note of something and that we confirm one another in the value we place on it. If I were to put myself forward as a celebrant of the virtue of love I would have to be convinced of that virtue as possessing the greatest efficacy of all, so as to be able to consider it worthy of memorial attention.

And the more people I can get to join me, the greater will be the celebration, presumably, and the more effective will be the power-enhancement of my god. So join me to celebrate the continued existence of what I prize most highly, please, because that will help me to enjoy it in the future.

*

Everything we do can be turned into an art. That means that we do it exceptionally well. It also means that we aim for spontaneity. Spontaneous excellence attained for our faculty of celebration of our god, or of what we mean by the good, this is called religion as art. It compares to religion as ethical and moral behaviour and should not be confused with it. There is the celebration of the good on one side and the doing of it on the other. These are two different things, and quite independently of who your god is or what you mean by the good. If your god is the nation and your good nationality, then you will celebrate at national festivals or in any number of ways devised by people who think and feel like you, and you can, if you like, make an art out of this, which is ritual and repeated; you will even celebrate the nation of your choice on Sundays in a church building, perhaps, because when the minister or priest says "god" you will hear and feel "nation" and "nationality" and perhaps "nationalism". (The nationalism would be an aberration of

141

your art in the direction of artistry, which is an opinion-ated way of going about it. For every art that avoids or neglects creativity the aberration of artistry is unavoid-able.) And then, in addition to this celebration of your god, the nation, there is your ethical and moral behaviour in terms of this good. Anything that serves your nation, though it harms another, is moral behaviour in your eyes, and international affairs will elicit a sense of ethics from you, a sense of belonging to a corporate group.

Ritual and repetition are important ingredients of re-ligion as art. In the interest of spontaneous excellence we try to repress all those elements in ourselves that might hinder it. This has to do now with all art, not specifically with religion as art. The ritual and the repetition are means and expedients towards that end of spontaneous excellence in some department. Whether they work, or not is another question. In any case, where an art is at-tempted, ritual is invented so as to keep in check and to discipline certain subsidiary faculties that are considered to become disruptive so that the selected one might func-tion spontaneously and so that we might excel in that one. What happens next, this depends on our creativity; and whether or not something beyond this excellence happens, this depends on the nature of the art we prac-tice.

As yet we have not, as it were, qualified religion. The god I myself worship, and in reality, is the one intro-duced from within the Hebrew culture to all men, women and children by Jesus of Nazareth, and his identifying attribute would seem to be parental and charitable love. Religion as art would therefore amount, for me, to spon-taneously excellent celebration of that love, in the company of others who, like myself, are drawn to this human love and consider it worth celebrating. I would not have to go to any particular building set aside for this but any occasion and any place would do, just so long as there are others who are willing to join me in certain ritual practices that repeatedly work for me. I value very highly the ritual practice of conversation and find it quite easy to enter into conversation with others who are willing to practice, for that purpose, the ritual of standing or sitting down with me somewhere, of repeated question and answer, and I would require that the repartee be truthful and generous.

Such a celebration requires then, in my case, a certain amount of attentiveness and care because no one arrives at excellence by way of a mere repetition of empty rituals. Disturbing elements have to be kept out of the way, such as a closed mind and compulsive talking. Eventually, then, love wins out and flows spontaneously - as an art work. Various things must be well done by those who participate in the celebration. No one drifts into it and certainly no one can make things happen. The god we would celebrate comes vividly among us as soon as he knows that we are ready, not when we decide we are ready – that would be a way of putting it.

No use pretending that the ritual in any way guarantees the feast. What I mean by the feast is the presence of our god among us in mutual joy and gladness. The love feast is one of human dignity married with divine perception.

Where human beings meet to celebrate their god of love they do it religiously and artfully. Due to their doing it religiously they confirm in one another's presence that their god is one of caring love, and by doing it artfully they overcome, each in himself for himself and all others, all the hindrances to spontaneous love.

*

If I love my fellow man as myself, this too is religion, and if I make an art of that, considering it now as something of a different emphasis, in comparison to religion as love of god, I must come to the conclusion that any kind of truly communal act may be turned into ritual and repeated. This comes as a surprise to those who suppose that the sacramental quality of an act depends on the way we behave when we act. Sacramental is only that which contributes to the excellence of religious behaviour, so we may seek to make that contribution at will. If we do make it, there is no end to the freedom we may institute for others and for ourselves, because this time the spontaneous excellence is not of celebration but of cerebration, or brain-action, which is pursued in awareness. Not much is known yet about the voluntary use of the brain and much can be learned here. Our persistent use of our brain in the interest of love of our fellow men, women and children brings to bear an intense influence on our community in a way that will certainly surprise us and cause much joy. But when this faculty is developed artfully to the point of spontaneous excellence we are in the possession of the secret of perfect success. Thereafter we ask no more questions because our joy is complete.

*

This notion of religion as art is, of course, experimental. What it highlights is the extent to which we can im-

144

prove our outlook and vary our manner. At the centre of religion as art we have the concept of worship, and we do well to ask ourselves what it is in our conduct that corresponds to the idea of worship. We are like confused children if there is nothing of which we are inwardly in awe, nothing that outwardly makes us wonder. We may suppose we are liberated and enlightened when in fact we are deserted and cast out. Modern man has finally excommunicated himself and he would like to imagine the reward as freedom. There are a few who have followed the fashion but they are not at all happy with the result. They do not succeed in convincing themselves that they have made progress and one would like to extend to them as many opportunities as possible for beginning a new introduction of themselves to the reality they cannot discover for themselves. Without this new reality they must remain senseless and discontent.

Religion as art is an offer of such an opportunity. Ask yourself: "Who is my god?" and. "What does my fellow man, the one presently next to me, mean to me; not in theory but in fact and experience? How do I add to him? What are my habits for encouraging him to live rather than to die?"

A sincere reply to these questions is of the utmost importance. And we have to look to one another if the image of the good is not to remain an empty one. We have to look to the one next to us for joining with us in genuine community, especially for the time being. In our minds we carry, perhaps, monstrous schemes for recognition and acknowledgment, while the person next to us remains totally indifferent to us. Our humanism flourishes while our humanity dries up. Religion pursued as an art frees for us the twin faculty of celebration and cerebration, so that we learn to cut through all those stultifying deposits on our consciousness that prevent us from seeing who we are and what we amount to – as though we were atoms in space.

* * *

21. Religion as Deed

Religion as feeling or experience can be talked about, but nothing appeals to us there once we have looked deep into the abyss between our individuality and the world. The bottomless pit, devoid of echo, swallows any amount of religious feeling and sentiment and leaves us teetering on the edge with our teeth chattering and nowhere to go for relief. And all the concepts in our brain and in the world combined can amount to a grand representation of what religion should amount to but we remain divorced from one another and separate from the God we define.

As soon as we look at religion as something we can do, we are not any more worried about being at fault or in error, but our shortcomings challenge us. Suddenly we experience for the first time a depth in ourselves from which impulses rise that are strong and self-evident, and our being here among others begins to make sense. A central truth springs to mind, namely, that we are made as we are made so that we will learn to depend on one another. We are not to be good, but to do good. We are not to be religious, but to do religion.

A proud self-sufficiency is a killer of religion, and yet we must learn that we exist and that in fact we are someone, before we can turn to another and offer an exchange.

Just that exchange has been long undervalued. It makes me shudder when I think for how long I ignored, that reality lay in community and not in individuality. Now I realize that to ask another his opinion or to enquire into his state of mind is not an exercise in mere curiosity but a door opened in myself by myself. To enquire honestly and respectfully is a substantial act in itself, whatever the response and whether or not there is one. Upon this point we may expend some contemplation. By looking to you for a contribution of yourself I give credit to your existence, I say: "Not only I, but you too exist," and in that little act lies a world of essential generosity. Of course I may yet have to learn to deal with your response, but once I have arrived on the communal level, those skills soon develop.

If we were to aim our education at children in a specifically religious manner, so that religion should be the chief gain of our efforts, we would probably begin by asking them personal questions, thereby showing them how to do that, so that they might imitate, and then ask us and one another questions. In the asking lies the virtue; the response is optional.

Good morning, children. Leslie, I wonder what you have in your schoolbag today, its bulging."

"Nothing."

"Jenny, can you hear me back there?" "Yes, I can."

"Will you tell us what you saw on the way to school today?"

"Nothing."

"My head spins. I wish I were so tall that my head peered out over the top of this building. George, you look lonely. Do you think that it's right for a person to be lonely?"

"I don't know."

The impartial bystander imagines the teacher must by now be frustrated because of the 'lack of response'. But quite on the contrary; what the teacher is doing is opening himself personally to the children, and he is doing it in spite of the lack of the sort of response one might suppose he desired. He refuses to provoke, to pry, to seduce, to chasten. He is not disappointed or resentful or sarcastic, because he knows what he is doing. It won't be long before articulate responses plentifully flow, but then he will not change his tactics. His enquiries will be spontaneous, sincere, intelligent and to the point. Any anger or indifference that wells up in him he immediately absorbs and his vision remains clear.

If it should happen now that suddenly the tables are turned and the children imitate what he did by asking questions, he keeps in mind the purpose of the exercise, which is not that he comes up with the most clever answer but that he honours the personality of the child. He does that in himself, for in himself, not out there, does the child as a person make a sensible impression. His most apt response may be lengthy or nothing at all:

"Why are you a teacher?"

"It's important for me to do."

"Why don't you get a job that pays more?"

"I don't much like jobs. Whenever a job comes along, I try to do it as quickly as possible so that I can get on with something else."

"Does it make you mad when we're noisy?"

"Noisy? Yes, sometimes. I wish it didn't."

His last response was nearly facetious, but he caught himself in time.

*

A personal question can also be directed to god, and here, too, it's the asking that counts. My inner disposition becomes interrogatory, and usually I have neither words nor thoughts nor feelings at the ready, and my attitude is that of a child towards a trusted parent. Did I say that religion, for me, is a doing? It takes a lot of inward doing, of doing within myself, before my attitude is as I want it and my disposition is as I know it must be if I am to get results. Because religion, as a doing, is all about results, and the primary results are to do with my mind, soul and strength; with whether or not I realize that as I ask I get what I ask for. Now if that is not a doing I don't know what is. In order to get the result I want, such as for example a more creative capacity in my work or a more productively patient approach to those I teach, I have to believe, or realize, or acknowledge, that the asking and the receiving are one and the same. If that makes no sense, then why not start with that, and ask that this should make sense.

If you can find nothing religious to do, at any time of the day, anywhere, within yourself, then there you have your first thing to do. Ask that your present mature re-

149

sponsibility to god and your fellow man should in some manner be revealed to you. And know that while you ask, it is in fact being revealed to you, even if at that moment you cannot yet put your finger on it. Suddenly, later on, it may pop into your mind, such as: "Yes, of course, my life is too hasty, I must do my work in a spirit of rest." or: "Come to think of it, there is a certain hollowness in myself, something dishonest, just waiting to be fulfilled as soon as I ask."

Religion is that sort of doing. With practice we can get inventive. A lot of traditional misconceptions have to be laid to one side. I can say 'prayer', or 'meditation', or 'practicing the presence of god', or 'fellowship', 'worship' etc. and I may mean something trivial, sensual, self-serving, or else something that gets worthwhile things done and makes good things happen. You don't know. But then there is no need for you to judge. You mind your own business. Within the secret domain of your personal conscientiousness you can do an infinite number of things that are immediately useful for all of us, that are never boring because never merely repetitive. Eventually you will even express your religious doing more outwardly, but that will come almost of itself. I ask right now that this will be so in your case.

* * *

22. Religious Education

It's a strange way of putting it, 'Religious Education', and maybe symptomatic in itself of a malaise of our culture. I nearly wrote: '..of a cultural malaise'. That would compare to 'religious education'. Are we to educate our children religiously? Well, only for two hours every week.

The rest of the time: well, not religiously, but ... deprived? depraved?

Nonsense. Of course no one means anything like that by religious education, by R.E. But don't ask me what people do mean, because when I asked them, the explanation sounded like everything from clownish entertainment to precepts of a creed drilled into them. Seduction seems to play a role, and superstition is not exactly frowned upon. One means well and succeeds in being meaningless. Worst of all, religion is trivialized and the truth is made suspect, - quite incidentally of course.

It's a novelty, bringing religion and education within the confines of one concept like this. I find there are, very basically, two attitudes towards religion. Some people are religious while others practice a religion. My own sympathies gravitate entirely towards the first lot. I practice no religion, but I am religious. I am religious in the sense that I know that I cannot be good but that I can do good. I am religious in that I believe that due to my action and passion others can be helped. Finally I am religious in that I harbour in myself an abiding and ever increasing respect for creation and in that I consider the world and all human beings in it as amazingly interesting and eminently worthwhile.

I have my doubts about those who practice a religion because they seem to me to want to manufacture a substitute reality rather than taking an interest in reality as is. I get the feeling that they do this either because they are too much in haste, so that they don't give reality a chance to reveal itself to them, from behind mere appearances, or else they are too lazy, so that they don't make the needful

151

effort to fight their way past their own prejudices in order to seek reality out. Diligent patience, responsible perseverance – a somewhat less than reverential attitude towards self and an earnest search for real value – does the advocate of a religion have any actual time or desire for these? And who is there, among those who adhere to a religion, who does not say, at best: "All religions may have something valuable about them, but mine is more than just another religion!" One feels inclined to ask: "Why? Because you chose it? Or because you were brought up in it?" And that's to ignore those who say: "Mine is the only true religion and I'm ready to murder you to prove it," and those on the other side who remain blissfully indifferent to the difference, because let's face it, they couldn't care less as long as they are allowed to belong to the club. Whether they wield it or are members of it, the club is usually a real issue for them.

What saddens me deeply is the tragic spectacle of those who have it in them to be religious, but the door has been locked for them by the institutional 'keepers of the keys'. They are the victims of religions. They have come to hate hypocrisy, lukewarmth, all manipulation of minds for the sake of uniformity, ecstasy and hierarchy, so that everything to do with religions has become invidious to them, while their own true self and soul remain locked.

These are the ones I would initially single out for 're-ligious education'. They cannot help themselves and they need to be drawn out of a complex of obnoxious inner circumstances. Something must be done for them because they cannot of themselves ever ask for it. Sometimes even children are among them. Usually they are grown-ups who have not yet become mature because of that particular hang-up concerning the truth of their own human nature. Of course they are ahead of those who embrace hypocrisy and toe the party line; for them nothing can be done for the time being.

*

The question that presents itself to me, sometimes painfully, is: how can I help someone be religious who is not able to be religious? How can I get him to see that he has in himself all the prerequisites for a meaningful existence and a rich and rewarding life, including complete joy, perfect happiness and great pleasure? Because most people suppose that the means to their ultimate satisfaction lie outside and somehow beyond their individual and communal existence. They either over-reach themselves and live beyond their means or else they lie back and wait for something to come to them from 'there'. Such is the profile of irreligion.

Now the educator can see that irreligion is not only a case of mistaken identity and of the wrong path taken, but also of pleasure derived from all these various short-circuits and shots in the dark and lost causes. The educator, who knows great pleasure, would not give a fig for all these little pleasures even if they were piled for him high as a mountain, and yet he can observe how their supposed enjoyment, plus the anxiety over the possible loss of it and the hankering after more of it, prevents people from coming to any workable terms with what he, the educator, calls simple, concrete reality. It's as if a sick man came to a doctor and said: "I know I am ill and I want to be cured, but don't ask me to get rid of the cause of my illness. Just make me feel good, don't ask me to change my approach to life."

And there are in fact a great many irreligious educators, or impostors, who are both willing and able to do just that. They will take away your appetite but leave you with your habit of chewing on stones. They will get rid of your pain for you but leave you your habit of injuring others and yourself. They have a good time of it, usually, because theirs is a popular pursuit.

The genuine educator, by comparison, sets himself the less facile task of weaning you away from your bad habits even as he shows you a few good ones. But then his success depends equally on you. The magician can touch you with his wand and presto, you seem cured, while in truth you are worse off, because now you have lost not only your health, but even the indication of you sickness. The doctor extends health to you and encourages you to reach out for it. If you don't reach out, there is absolutely nothing he can do for you. But if you do reach out, he can do it all.

And there we have come to the single important difference between the educator of immature adults and the educator of children. What I mean by 'reaching out' is something that adults must do before they can get ahead and something that children cannot do. Or, to put it the other way round, the educator must do it for children, but he cannot possibly do it for adults. At a certain age, give or take five or ten years, something in a human being clicks into place, and then he becomes capable of authenticity and liable to egocentricity. Prior to that he is not capable of authenticity and not liable to egocentricity.

Prior to that, certain things must be done for him. The educator says: He must be raised, he must be brought up.

The adult - the human being in whom that certain something has clicked into place - cannot be brought up or raised. He either grows, creatively and fruitfully, in accordance with this maturity, or he lapses into egocentricity and self-consciousness and thereby becomes - immature. Even an immature adult cannot be raised or brought up, to maturity, or to greater or full maturity. His immaturity does not imply that he has gone back to a state prior to the time when that certain something clicked into place. We might tell him to 'grow up', but we cannot raise him or bring him up. The main point is, that an adult, in order to be rid of any immaturity at all, has to reach out for something. The educator can show it to him, but he cannot do for him what he can do for a child. A child, again, cannot be immature, cannot be self-centred or authentic. A child must be brought up or raised.

*

All effective education is religious, but especial emphasis can be placed on that aspect of it which brings home to a human being his relation to the good and to others in terms of love. Certainly no one should be instructed in one religion or in another. If a teacher introduces to his pupils some facts about the life of Jesus of Nazareth, then he should do this in the same way as when he speaks of Shakespeare, of Napoleon or of Albert Schweitzer. He should explain why he talks about this person at all and then he should keep in mind that all human beings have a common destiny, are equally deserving of respect and that we know them not by their fame, in other words by what others say or said about them, but by their works. Unless a teacher feels he can estimate the works of a person he should not introduce that person to children. And then he should speak of those persons either in a spirit of love or not at all. A great deal can be said about one person in spirit of love, but not so much about another. When we make the spirit of love our guide, we educate or teach more religiously than ever, and then it becomes possible even to teach love.

In such a thing as religious education, then, the spirit of love is augmented, because it becomes in itself the object and the subject of the lesson in which the pupils participate. All teaching must go on in a spirit of love, whether one aspect of the world is highlighted or another. But when love itself is highlighted, then we can speak of religious education.

Imagine teaching love in the spirit of love. Suddenly that which is talked about comes together with the reason for talking about anything in the first place. Subject and object coincide. Whether adults or children are to be religiously educated, one appeals to human nature in human beings in order to reveal to the human being not the goodness of his nature, which would always be a delusion, but his natural instinct for love, his desire to love and be loved. To the extent that this instinct had been blinded it can be revised. To the extent that this desire has been twisted or thwarted it can be set back on course again and revitalized.

*

The difficulty, in the classroom, with religious education, centres, then, on what one means by religion, given that education is understood correctly as creative action. Where a promise is implicit in the teacher's approach, a promise to the pupil to the effect that sooner or later he will be isolated by love in such a way that he will seem to himself quite incomprehensible and that the world will seem to him an insurmountable obstacle - and where that promise is implicit in such a way that the pupil begins to sense the purpose in that isolation because he is being lovingly prepared for it in a variety of modes and manners - and finally where that promise is also one of eventual fulfilment, in the sense that out of his own human nature will rise, for the pupil, his own creative personhood, as insecurity and anger dwindle, so that he will understand and be capable of overcoming - there we can truly speak of religious education, because the teacher understands the workings of love, the operation and effect of it as it influences all human beings at all times whether they take advantage of this or not.

The origin of personality in a human being is a great mystery. What we mean by someone's personhood either exists or does not exist, and to any educator, teacher or instructor the existence of personhood, potential or actual, is of primary interest. The aim of all education is maturity, and maturity does not come about by itself. What does come about is a moment in time - and this has to be expressed in the negative - after which the human being is liable to immaturity. Prior to that he was amenable to being raised; after that he is at liberty to create or to destroy, and any education on his behalf after that depends upon his willing co-operation, on his intention to improve. This should come as welcome news to any adult - I mean the suggestion that he can instigate his own education - but most of us resent being reminded of it, because as soon as we are outwardly grown up we like to think of ourselves as finished and prefer to concentrate on our rights rather than on our opportunities. The educator concentrates on opportunities for creative personality and we can consider religious education as a special effort, by the educator, on behalf of human individuality in a confused world.

* * *

23. Religious Instruction

At a parent evening, recently, the topic of 'religious instruction' came up. I would like to explain how I feel and what I think about the possible relevance of such a thing as Religious Instruction, or instruction in religion, to the up-bringing and education of children after the age of eleven or twelve years, and I take as my starting point the question: How do I suppose my own eleven-year-old son might be helped, by adults who take an interest in his growth, if those adults, nowadays, in Northern Ireland, were to try to stimulate his growth specifically in terms of religion as understood by teachers either trained in creative education or at least in hopeful sympathy with it.

There are so many unknown factors in that equation that I feel like giving up before I start. What comes to mind at the outset is: Why should I ask teachers to contribute to something that might go on quite successfully at home? It seems already like a salutary thing, in our NI environment, not to make an issue out of Religion. Home influence in that direction is bound to do good. As long as at the same time a positive example is set. Parents who feel alright about spending only a hasty half hour per day with their children, parents who don't, perhaps, even care much about such an environment as a home, in comparison to a house, might follow a good instinct if they entrust to teachers even the 'religious' up-bringing of their children. They will say: "Our children have no proper home or family with us, everything is so up and down and torn to pieces, let them therefore benefit from a school where a bit of community spirit reigns and where the teachers have a valid centre to their lives." That secret instinct is to be respected in those parents. They are going through trials typical to the late twentieth century, when traditions lie in tatters and a new reality is waiting to be built - and, let's be realistic, the new reality is not going to be built by those who shrink away from those trials into the backwaters of a bankrupt culture but by those few who have themselves experienced those trials and have courageously, if somewhat dazed, come through.

If I myself have learned something by coming through some of those trials it is that a variety of points of view is essential. The new reality can not be embraced in a belief system, in a creed, in a religion. Characteristic of it is, that it has to be approached with an attitude for which I can find no better name than the communal attitude. First my own point of view has to be authentic, there is no escape from that. Unless I have learned to feel and think for myself I have no ground to stand on. But then that genuine and originally sound point of view has to be recognized by me as being one among a possible many, so that conversation becomes essential. I can think of nothing more important to me than the encouragement I can offer to others to make up their own minds, so that I can have someone else to relate to, to exchange views with – not so that we can all arrive at the same opinion but because there is real life to be gained from it. While I anxiously defend my position, or the position of my particular guru or false messiah, I gain the opposite to life. But of course if my position is real, I have no desire to defend it but I want to share with those around me the benefits of it. Anyone who challenges it is welcome with open arms, because obviously he wants to know, and I want to know too, and there's knowledge in communication.

I believe I have inadvertently indicated one aspect of what I mean by religion.

If I turn the problem around, I have to admit that I would like to see my child spend time in the company of grown-ups who know how to take pleasure in being morally responsible for one another, who are aware of the benefits of being able to forgive one another, who would rather turn the other cheek than get their own back and who prefer to feel bad rather than good if once again they haven't done so; who are broad minded, tolerant of other points of view, honest with themselves and helpful to others. If I thought there was a way of drawing my children's attention to such a behaviour in a special way, in addition to what constant personal example can accomplish, I would be in favour of it.

Finally it seems to me that religion, fundamentally as love of god and neighbour, cannot be taught to children, as a separate curriculum subject. However if anyone can help my child be more, rather than less loving, under a variety of circumstance, that would be great. Certainly it should be possible to teach children how to love, and between their tenth and seventeenth year it should be possible to prepare them for adolescence when a multitude of sensations that are unfamiliar to them surface in them and they are faced, time and again, with the tricky choice between love as an often painful accomplishment and lovely infatuation as a corruption.

On reflection it seems to me that instead of contemplating instruction in religion we might consider instruction in love. Damage is done to the human natural affectionate disposition of very young children by those around them; teachers may take the responsibility for undoing some of that damage. Contemporary influences of hatred, falsehood and ugliness confirm older children in their suspicion that life is at best a game and reality the trick of getting your own way; teachers may take the initiative to counteract some of that influence. Love, as something that is done and not merely experienced, can undo all damage, can counteract all wickedness and even turn it to good.

Morality without love is nothing more than a stick and a carrot. But where love is learned, morality is just about implied. We see around us all too much religion without love, and history is littered with the effects of Religions. But where love is practiced, Religions become irrelevant and religion is a fact in any case. So if we start with love, morality and religion can be taken for granted.

From love flow humility, mercy and kindliness. In love reside respect, obedience, orderliness, excellence and service. On account of love we are honest, forthright, forgiving, strong even in our weakness and powerful.

The desire to love, actively, secretly, even heroically, becomes a pressing issue with adolescence. How many adolescents have been brought up and educated so that they can begin to express themselves in such a loving manner? How many are equipped with forms of thought and feeling into which they can now pour their awakening instincts, decently, with dignity and joyful trust in their own abilities as they look towards the future?

At a creative school, teachers know that if the child is not loved, the pupil makes no real progress, no matter how well he can spell or subtract. Love is always somehow part of the equation. It must be, or the education itself becomes hollow. But then love itself can become a hollow word; even a 'four letter word'.

Now it seems to me that just as the child under ten or eleven years of age could not gain at all from having love talked about, because it must have love as a live environment, so do adolescents need to be able to discuss love; more fundamentally, they need to be able to think about it, to become familiar with the idea and conception of it, to understand more and more the laws and principles of it, the communication and misunderstanding of it. So the time of pre-adolescence, between eleven and fifteen, should perhaps be viewed as a preparation for adolescence, when the need to express love actively and creatively becomes pressing. Sexuality, for example, has become such a burning issue, and such a pitfall for so many of our youngsters, because no other expression of love seems left except this drive, which is perceived as at least natural – while it lasts.

I fear that we betray young people if we say that we base their education on a knowledge of them as becoming human beings but then we neglect to any degree at all the active core and essential creativity of them, which is love in its infinite aspects, from affectionate adoration of god as father, through deep and attentive care for one another, to sexuality, marriage and procreation. Human natural affection itself today is so shot through with cynicism and disappointment that any corrective at all would seem worthwhile, even if one were only to bring this fact itself to conscious awareness.

To get down to a very few practicalities: For preadolescent children over the age of ten, say, it would seem suitable to hear various issues connected with love, morality and religion intelligently and knowledgably talked about, within a context adapted to their age and present state of culture. What has to be kept in mind is that due to unavoidable mass media abuse, love (religion and morality) are continually talked about, but destructively, in a trivializing and demeaning manner, in association with guilt, violence, vengeance, obscenity, etc. A corrective would be to talk about them in a context of magnanimity, creativity and good will. And yet one would of course 'talk about them' indirectly. I am thinking of stories, plays both read and acted out, dramatizations represented or improvised, gesture and mime exploited and explored. (Imagine a group of five eleven-year-olds inventing a mime sequence for illustrating the difference between gratitude and ungrateful behaviour. Think of fourteen-year-olds writing letters to imaginary friends forgiving them for an unkindness or accusing them of a wickedness they themselves have perpetrated.)

The possibilities of success (and failure!) of such a venture are endless. Immense amounts of work would have to be put in by suitable people to explore these possibilities. Then there would have to be a willingness to try out one thing after the other, to start small, on a modest scale, learning step by step.

If I let my mind wander I can think of more reasons I think that at a standard school it wouldn't have much of a chance, but at a creative school the appeal to the child's nature is already implicit, so here we should perhaps ask: can we afford not to try it?

Think of the effect on boys and girls of a dialogue between two adults who first argue about their individual ways of looking at the same picture and then hug each other. Or what about children who 'walk', in front of others, courageously, boastfully, cowardly, anxiously – . Or mock jury trials are acted out to condemn those who are accused of rebelliousness, of stealing a sweet, of being kind to a dirty beggar in front of 'decent' people. Symbolic stories could be written to illustrate the good effect of a kind word at the right moment, of patience on the one who is patient, of an honourable deed in spite of crowd disapproval. I say specifically: symbolic stories, not moralizing allegories. Short, relevant passages could be read, without further explanation, from the great literature of the world, from the Old and New Testament, centred on a theme that would be obvious only to the instructor.

No matter how many 'venues' can be dreamt up, however, all would depend on who does the instructing. Such people would above all have to have life experience of their own, and therefore true insight into the importance of love, not to mention a commitment to teaching. They would be able to appreciate that love is not always welcome as a pleasant thing, that some, in fact, have been crucified for loving - which makes it an all the more important thing to do.

I feel I have barely scratched the surface of something here and look forward to discussing it with anyone who sees anything useful in it that might be implemented in a school, under whatever name. If it were worked out with due deliberation and foresight, it could be presented to parents for inspection and comment.

* * *

24. Self-Examination,
Communion and Community

We live at least inwardly, alert to the changes here, and aware of two things: of our liability to evil and of our functional virtue.

If we do not live inwardly, we cannot live outwardly. The inward life must really be discovered and those who look for it will in fact find it. Once the inner life is sufficiently developed it bears fruit as outward activity. Then we can say that we even live outwardly. Those who know merely the outside of everything do not try to confuse us, they merely adhere to the terms they are left with, and these they structure as best they might. Our task is not to confuse them either, but to live nevertheless.

Our first impulse to self-examination is usually in response to challenges presented by those who insist on a reality made up of the outside of everything. We say with justification that their reality is extinct. What they call reality is extinction. We not only have a right to describe their reality on our own terms, but we are wise to do so, for the sake of our own clarity. It would seem childish for us to pretend that extinction mistaken for reality is not prevalent in the world. A suicidal impulse sways him who has been touched inwardly by the life, only to entertain after all the possibility that extinction might be real.

Extinction, especially planned, systematic extinction, confuses us because appearances look so right, even good but the hollowness escapes us, so we experience, in ourselves, something like resentment, or envy, actually because we cannot match in terms of real, inwardly rooted life, what gives itself the appearance of such reality out there.

This resentment, or envy, draws our attention to our inward state and we say: "What is this remarkable complicity of my soul with extinction? Why am I moved to despair in the absence of all good reason for it?" By this time the envy and the resentment have drawn our attention to themselves, away from that seeming perfection, that systematic extinction 'out there' and we are like someone going through hell. We may know we are being purified. We may understand that we could not possibly experience such an envy or resentment, or now such despair, if we had not the instinct for truth, the capacity for real inner life. "Our inner grief at being not among the extinct" - this says it all.

For a while we mistake the extinct for the elect, then we catch ourselves on. We mourn for our lost extinction until the absurdity of this occurs to us, or until we take proper cognizance of our instinct for the truth.

Then our self-examination has begun. We ourselves must begin it, again and again, until it becomes a good habit. The correct interpretation of that grief, of that despair or that resentment and envy is at stake. These are accidental manifestations of our self. They are our self in the flesh. Alright, so on account of them our attention was drawn in the right direction, but do we have to wait again and again for this to happen or does the time come when we say: "I do not need grief and despair to point me on the way. I know the direction now, and I will set out voluntarily."

So we set out. Our instinct for truth becomes a live desire. We search, not waiting until circumstances overwhelm us. All the same, we are beginners, and then we are only beginners, so we flirt with extinction. We want the best of both worlds, namely the true peace and the false glitter. We try to serve two masters. Heavens, it comes over us, we do not necessarily even intend it. (Woe to him who intends it.) So once again there is grief, despair, envy and resentment, any combination or permutation of these, and we are quite wretched, because perhaps we imagined that just the once in harness would do to make us immune. But not so. Due to our self we are once again thoroughly unhappy. How can we dissolve our self? Self-examination will do the trick. We do well to keep it handy. Without it we lose track of our beginning towards the inward truth. We commit all sorts of nonsense and lose track, so much so that we cannot find the beginning, and that is real wretchedness. No hell like in sight of paradise. Perhaps we suppose that our one taste of freedom is a liberty and a license. The licentious libertine has tasted true freedom, but then he lost track and - intended extinction? Even if he does not intend it, he is still in a fix.

Self-examination implies a perception, by me, of my negative, or rather of my unproductive, inner states (at the time they may seem quite positive to me) and an understanding of these states in the light of the inward truth that makes them possible in the first place. An extinct individual commits nonsense without being in the least put out by it.

We ought to mention at this stage that the modern individual, as usual, goes halfway: instead of letting these unproductive inner states sway him to the life within him he tries to get rid of them, because he finds them unpleasant, or he tries to make something out of them, if he finds them convenient and pleasant. He becomes a therapist or a supernaturalist. He comes to the sign that says: "this way to the life" and he studies the spelling or mass produces the sign. His perception of his self is not true but ambiguous, so he never gets past it. Nearly two-thousand years of modernity have ingrained a tradition of halfwayism, and this entire tradition must go the way of all flesh that refuses good spirit.

By means of self-examination I dissolve my self entirely every time and am ready for communion.

The essential act of communion lays bare the inner truth of my being. I am truthfully able to say that I am. But the origin of the truth in myself is not myself, and this is the difficult lesson to learn here. My communion is initially a union with the truth, so I must have a notion of the truth. If I did not, I would forever be divided against myself. The search for truth and the hope of finding it is not, in human beings, an accidental fancy but as organic a function as sleeping and breathing. A human being cannot not seek the truth without ceasing to be. The truth is the way we all fit into time and space and into the fellowship of men, women and children. How we fit in, this is the search for the truth. Human beings do not automatically 'fit in'. They fit in inasmuch as they seek the truth, and those who seek it, find it. The seeking and the finding are one. Besides, the seeking of the truth is a joy, so human beings are by definition joyful beings, complete insofar as they seek and find the way in which they belong to the universe and the universe to them.

No one can point at the truth but we perceive it. Our perception of it is communal. In order to understand this we must know that this organic activity of human beings is productive of a result. Due to my seeking of the truth I accumulate something which I then need to share, to give and to impart. We can think of communion as work, and we can think of it as the work that is perfectly characteristic of a human being. We are not talking about something here that has to be added on to human beings or that they need to seek outside of themselves, but the work of communion and the ready fruits of this work are germane to human being, and part and parcel of the way we are while we truly are. This communal action would not occur to me unless I had you or another one in mind for whom I were doing it. Again, this is perfectly human natural and can be seen as the normal functioning of our

169

human virtue or conscious essence. I commune for the-sake of community. I seek the truth for the sake of a few, several or many. I desire to find my position in the scheme of things and persons so that you and others may benefit from this. Doing it for that reason satisfies me completely, and no wonder, because that is the way I am made. During my association with you my self may very well have moved to the forefront. An act of self-examination is immediately followed by the work of communion so that community might replace society. I presuppose here that our meeting was not right away communal but social. Community with you is therefore my ambitious goal, and I do not allow myself to be put off by any unproductive states in myself, but I understand them completely and move out of their way so that my self dissolves and the work of communion can begin, otherwise I have nothing to pass on to you.

Community can be seen as human beings working for one another like this, with no look to any reward except their true status and position as human beings.

And yet it would be a mistake to assume that any part of this work is sacrificial. The nature of sacrifice is always one-sided. A man exerts himself for some outward or inward gain. In the case of communion, there is no exertion and the gain is whole. As soon as we are, truly, we are here and now in contact with one another and only an extinct tradition of knowledge can interfere with that insight. As soon as I am, truly, I participate in that which you are when you truly are. I participate in it and I have the benefit, the good fit, of it. Learning to be is therefore of crucial importance and of singular advantage.

And the progression from being to being someone is gradual. The so-called identity crisis is merely the process of shedding that extinct self. We repeat: the patient and still act of being in truth, communally, is progressive. There is accumulation and gain. Original faculties come into being. Organic functions come into being. This has to be known, otherwise we stray into vanity and desuetude. There is a central awareness, during the course of actual communion, that it leads somewhere, namely to community. By way of communion we get somewhere, we are on the way. This is the way, that we do not get stuck in the contemplation of our navel or in the sorrow for the lack of a sign, but we grow towards community. We do well to continue to know that, to hold that knowledge in our mind, because that ongoing and persistent knowledge is essential to our growth into community. We grow into and towards community. Sufficient being turns into becoming. I accumulate human being and I become - a human being. For a while I know what I am, namely human, and then, because I know that this is so, I become a human being. Human being turns into human beings. Communion enters community. Grasp that and you have what it takes. Work only with this knowledge and never look for signs, neither for signs of progress, nor for signs of arrival, for all such signs are extinct while your work is faithful instinctively. (Assume that instinct is the prerogative of animals and you have gone to the dogs.)

Community is a natural and spontaneous reaching out to other human beings and to potential human beings, and for those who espouse extinction we set the impunitive example. By impunitive I mean that there is not even

171

the slightest recrimination or accusation in our conduct among those who adhere to society and in our behaviour towards those who know only to associate but not to commune. Our exemplary conduct in society without being part of it is, once again, as much in our own interest as to the benefit of those members of society, so there is nothing of personal sacrifice or such-like for the sake of those who are devoid of perception. Our example is for them the very best. And we set that example not by way of compromise with the ways of extinction, flirtatious and seductive, nor by setting up imperialist organizations of our own, in the hope of 'beating them at their own game'. The very notion of 'them and us' is already a sign for us that we have strayed from the truth, in need of self-examination.

The distinction between community and a community is such that once again the two can not be separated, not any more than communion and community. Let them know us by our works, not by our collective labels. Know them by their conduct and behaviour, not by their jargon, their secret signs and their group psyche. A community in no time can turn into a pseudo-society, and is then justly mocked by those who hate the truth. Once I have lost my inward and practical link with the truth I am ethically adrift and morally hollow. The taste has gone out of the seasoning. I deserve to be cast into the wind. If community is to spring up, the seed of it that lies buried in the human psyche must die. With the psyche away, soul thrives.

* * *

25. Supporting a Creative School

(050295)

The health, the moral health, of an organization like a school dedicated to creative teaching, is a precarious thing. There are many influences that work against a harmonious growth, against that gradual, organic development, that is itself, of course, an element unique to such an institution. It would seem crucial, in regard to such a school, to keep in mind its special status, the very original conception of it.

Even the high ideal of the founder of the school is sometimes not more important, when we contemplate the overall meaning of a creative education approach, than the will and desire of those parents who make this out-of-the-ordinary commitment to the upbringing of their children. The fact that these parents think about their children in a very certain way, that they choose to make an issue of something that would otherwise perhaps follow a mundane routine, this deserves to be looked at carefully. The founder of any type of creative education can only tap into an urgency that already exists among people, he cannot reproduce something that he alone but no one else cares about.

So what I am suggesting here is that the moral health of a creative education establishment, its ethical integrity and sound sense of purpose, will improve or decline in proportion to the quality of the interest that parents take in the actual education, in this uncommon and rather special education, which they want for their offspring.

The first reaction to such a statement is often: That's the affair of the teachers. Parents must trust that teachers

173

know what they are doing. Parents are not trained, not equipped intellectually, to comment. – This is quite correct, so far as it goes. This is why we emphasize the quality, not the degree, of interest that parents might take, that they must take, in the education they desire for their children. There is no question that teachers should be left to their devices in the classrooms, to the slow, thorough unfolding of their skills, to the painstaking construction of the all-important teacher-pupil relationship. There is however an abiding and sensitive question that this highly imaginative work should be, by parents, taken blithely for granted. Those of us who have ever tried to achieve something, know how it feels to be 'supported' by people who barely understand what we have in mind. I consider that such unwitting support operates, in the long run, negatively. Hollow encouragement actually undermines, in a subtle fashion, the will to persevere. Ignorant praise is worse than a lack of recognition.

The crucial element, therefore, is knowledge and understanding. And before we take a wrong turning here, let's emphasize: we mean knowledge and understanding of what we ourselves, as parents, want for our children. I would even go so far as to say that it would take several parents to get together on this. The thing to be known and understood here exists on a level more basic and more substantial than any routine and standard method of teaching and learning. It has meaning, this education we have in mind, not solely and exclusively within the context of the individual, but specifically in the realm of the communal. Each one of us by ourselves can only have a dim notion of it. We sense perhaps that we would like our children to have something we ourselves missed. We

174

nourish a fond hope that their natural desire to learn will not be stifled, like ours - and there it stops. Not until we make a sustained effort to communicate what we have in mind can we really come to terms with the truth of it.

Creative education is not like a product that can be advertised so that a demand for it is created. The demand has to come first, and from parents who know and can say in detail why they make that demand. Some of us feel that creative education is such a crucial issue that we would dearly like to suggest it to others, as something to consider and to take up. How can we do that unless we learn to articulate what we mean by it? At the point of origin of any successful creative education venture stands a group of insightful parents who have joined in their wish to come to terms with something they feel should be done and might be done. The insight has to continue and grow over the years.

Teachers can thrive within such an informed environment. The strength on which creative teachers can draw resides in the enlightened hearts and minds of the parents who send their children to them. We need to instil in ourselves an abiding dissatisfaction with our bad habit of taking creative education for granted, as though it were, after all, something else to be supplied by faceless experts in our absence. Teachers who practically dedicate their existence to the development of young human beings towards a genuine maturity will thrive and be effective while they have some guarantee, some confidence, that the parent knows and understands what they do, but they are bound to wilt or burn out in an atmosphere that is not authentically appreciative, or largely indifferent.

Even if enough creative teachers were about, they could not function in an atmosphere of indifference, or worse, of hollow good intentions, where wishful thinking and a few trite phrases are supposed to serve. It's quite wrong, not to say reprehensible, for us to imagine that the education we look for from these teachers and that becomes ever more available from them is different only in degree from the standard, State invoked variety. The difference is radical. The creative education on offer is different in kind and impulse. But it can remain on offer only under certain conditions.

And those conditions must be supplied by parents inasmuch as they take the trouble to go a bit further than their initial decision to enrol their child, and insofar as they take pains to explore the reasons for their decision. Considering what is at stake and in view of the nature of the reward, an ongoing dialogue is required. The fruits of such a dialogue are bound to benefit in the up-bringing of our children at home too.

* * *

26. Teacher Training I

What is a teacher who has not the capacity of creative inwardness? What is a teacher who has not at his disposal a whole battery of means and devices for overcoming, in himself, negative reaction and destructive limitation?

An adult who walks into a classroom full of pupils defensively, hardened against insult and inconvenience, is not able to teach, not any more than if he strode in aggressively, with a mind to overcome, in pupils, all possible reaction and limitation. If he tries to protect his wilful self, in other words, he is no better off than if he attempts to impose it, because in neither case can he teach. He might be able to indoctrinate pupils, aggressively, or defensively he might be able to lure them out into the open where they are then bound to behave badly, but none of this has anything to do with teaching, which concept applies to a process of recognition that comes about, where the pupil becomes aware of himself and of the world, and of himself and others, in meaningful relationship.

Unless, in an adult, there exists at least a modicum of voluntary inwardness, he cannot possibly be expected to teach. There is plenty of accidental inwardness in all of us, because we shrink from the pain there and seek out the comfort. In a teacher some inwardness must be voluntary, and the more of it the better.

Now it's possible to test for this voluntary inwardness. Ask yourself, next time when something annoys you, could you just as readily accept the thing that causes you annoyance? Or if you catch yourself insisting on your right to something, such as your right to be heard or your right to silence, could you just as readily forego that right?

This is a test which reveals to us the beginnings or the absence, of a capacity for voluntary inwardness. I do not mean that you should be able to forego your right – let's call it your right to justice – because you cannot do anything about it anyway, since circumstances overwhelm you and you are bound to give in, but that you should simply be able to stop insisting even while it feels good to insist, even. while you are full of arguments, logical, rational or passionate, in support of your right to insist. The sore point here is, that only if you overcome your insistence on your right, even in some small way, can you be sure, initially, that your inwardness is actually voluntary and not accidental or cowardly.

By this I do not mean to suggest that all real voluntary inwardness must always somehow be preceded by such an act of self-overcoming. An accomplished teacher is able at a moment's notice to renew in himself the charitable space that is required for both active and passive teaching. The inexperienced adult, however, is liable to mistake a variety of states of being for voluntary inwardness, and for this reason a test is required. What if you merely indulge in an indolence of the soul? What if your so-called inwardness is nothing more than a callous indifference, into which you slipped habitually after disappointment and despair? What if you have nothing more to offer here than self-gratification and self-satisfaction, based on your definition of adult superiority? With the best of wills we cannot detect such states in ourselves unless we seriously examine ourselves as we act and behave. When doubt creeps in, this may be a healthy sign, because until now we may have been certain, but wrong.

*

The voluntary inwardness of a prospective teacher, once it exists as a practicable possibility, can be nurtured and trained.

We should not suppose now that an adult can be made to do things against his will. However his volition can be beneficially enlisted. If an adult is shown, by someone who knows how this voluntary inwardness is a fertile state of being, he will find this attractive and he will wish to fall in with it. Right away he must be shown how this fertile state of being can only exist in the interest of others. Calling it voluntary is therefore not enough unless the will we mean is good.

Can the adult extend good will towards others from his own base of fertile inwardness? Does he realize, that whatever he really does and what he truly brings about in this department, must be done, as it were, in secret? No one can tell from without that he does it. We can tell from without, however, that he must have been doing it when we are faced with the results.

Half the battle seems to be the realization that for every human adult there exists a state of inward being that is fertile and productive of results. A young adult is beginning to become familiar with this faculty of his volition and, depending on his up-bringing and education until then, he will either identify will exclusively with external attainment, such as: I want to earn more and more money; I want the good report of others; I will be a doctor, a mathematician, an engineer, etc.; or he will have discovered that his inner disposition and mood, his temperament, thought and feeling, may also be brought within the confines of a loving ambition and attainment, not in terms of control or manipulation, but productively and creatively. If the latter is the case, as one dearly hopes, then he has not far to go before he perceives how the way we succeed outwardly depends on the way we proceed inwardly, within ourselves and among one another. Knowledge and understanding of our individual and communal being must precede all worthwhile cognition and recognition of world.

Now it is within this realm of individual and communal inwardness that teacher training must go on We may compare it to the training of the stage actor, who must be able to relate to himself and to his fellow actors on the stage, during a performance, in such a way that the inward truth of a persona is exemplified. The teacher must, by comparison, be able to relate to himself and to his pupils in such a way that his own inward truth is exemplified.

First of all this inward personal truth must be discovered, and plenty of time should be set aside for this discovery tour. Modern man likes to pretend, and often he mistakes his habitual pretence for the genuine article. The prospective teacher may be guided through such a maze of pretence and even pretentiousness to the point where he makes contact, in himself and in his relationship with his guide and colleagues, with the fertile ground of his being. He will right away give evidence of this, contact in his outward behaviour, in the way he moves and speaks, and in the telling way he can be still and silent.

This contact with his inner truth is a crucial stage in the development of a teacher, and it should be celebrated. However, experience shows, that such a celebration does not need to be 'staged' but that it quite naturally breaks out, as though human nature were congratulating itself on having once again succeeded in breaking through into personal freedom. During every training session such a celebration may manifest itself, often mildly, but sometimes dramatically, as the trainee, due to special attention and effort, draws once again more intensively on his inner truth, though the first time is usually quite memorable.

Next comes the initiation and development, of inner faculties. These faculties spring spontaneously from the truthful ground of one's being as soon as, so to speak, sufficient room has been made for them. They are not caused or brought about by us, these faculties, and they are not extensions of will-power or mechanical effects of effort. They are gracefully initiated. Take, for example, such a simple faculty as vision, which includes and entails all our sense apparatus. The trainee is shown how to envision an environment for himself that is composed entirely of elements that occur to him at that moment, sparingly or in abundance. He is shown how to differentiate between invented and recalled data, and with increasing facility he can build for himself, on the spur of the moment, visual surrounding, that express and correspond to his being at that time. He does this for himself, but by the same token he does it for his fellow trainees and for his guide, who wish him well and observe what he does. In this way he becomes adept at creating a space that is empathetically conducive to communication.

After vision, the next faculty to be tackled might be imagination and fantasy. The trainee first describes a fresh set of visual surroundings and then, in that setting, he imagines and relates an event, on a very modest scale at first, and the guide always takes especial care to lead the trainee away from anything dishonest, disingenuous or merely repetitive. He prompts the trainee, to conduct him back to his true centre. He encourages the trainee to notice pressure, anxiety, insecurity and to welcome these in himself, as raw materials for further (transcendent) imagination and fantasy. Every trainee will show an aptitude for a different set of inward faculties. Eurhythmic behaviour and speech is a natural outcome and can then be enhanced. Awkwardness, reluctance or 'showing off' are not criticised but gently dissipated due to an emphasis on action and thought.

The guide proceeds loosely according to a plan but is always ready to co-operate with the creative spirit that soon shows itself more than eager to comply with a genuine good willingness on everyone's part to be surprised and to learn. The guide takes notes and these are separately discussed for a short time afterwards.

After vision, imagination and fantasy may come feeling and passion, then thinking and rational argument. When each trainee has made sufficient contact with his own voluntary inward being and has had some practice with an embodiment of three or four faculties, two trainees may be asked to work together in the creation of a communal space and in the exploration of some faculties as exercised and experienced during personal relationship.

All this is done in front of an 'audience' that is made up of the guide and the other. trainees. This 'audience' must understand that their own silent good will is of crucial importance, otherwise nothing of value is gained by them and the trainee's task becomes unnecessarily difficult.

The faculty of emotion is of especial importance in our day because unchecked intellect is fashionable these past two centuries, so that emotion has fled, as it were, into subterranean caves. What we take for emotion nowadays is usually in fact thwarted and abused emotion insisting on its natural rights or bitterly pleading its case. Eurhythmy as an art form is singularly suited to usher genuine human emotion from its hiding places by preparing for it an organic atmosphere of trust, free from criticism and from a judgmental or condemnatory influence. When a trainee discovers how eurhythmically he speaks and moves once he does so from his true centre of being, he soon adopts that speech and movement for a more permanent representation of his inwardness, for those around him. What appeared of its own free will (spontaneously) to his consciousness, he lifts up into awareness.

The actual curriculum of a creative teacher has to do, among other things, with his own awareness of his changing inner being and with his prompt and creative response to it. The awareness and the responsibility – that is to say: the ability to respond, by means of ordinary human faculties, to often unexpected changes in disposition, temperament and mood, in such a way so that creative progress is made, this is what at least half of teacher training must be about.

* * *

27. Teacher Training II

An actor has his script, a teacher his curriculum. If teaching is to be an art, or even creative, then the teacher is not interested in amassing knowledge. He knows that if something can be amassed, then it cannot be knowledge. During the past four centuries the search for something generally thought of as objectively verifiable knowledge has shown itself to be no more than an unregenerate attempt to exercise cupidity over a reality out there, that incidentally allows us to ignore our lack of reality in here. Any attempt at world conquest is accompanied by loss of soul, not only in the sphere of politics but in every arena of human endeavour, including 'education'.

The concept 'education as an art' begs the question: what is art? Artists are notoriously beset by demons from below, by 'powers and principalities' from above, and at times they flirt with these, at the risk of becoming addicted to them in dubious exchange for 'magical powers', for which the labels are changed from generation to generation in hopeless attempts to stay ahead of a scrupulous conscience.

World-historically, our present position is such that the artificial separation of objective from subjective knowledge, as witnessed by our distinction of sciences from humanities, has undergone a curious twist, in that the humanities, the supposed realm of subjective knowledge, have been demoralized by 'objective criticism', while the sciences, the proposed realm of objective knowledge, are being undermined by 'inarguable subjectivity'. A decent marriage of object and subject seems to be the only solution,

It would be totally inappropriate to demand that education should not be world-centred. What it should not be is this-world-centred. The insight required to understand what is meant by this is itself based on the knowledge that the end of this world is world without end. Such knowledge is not modern. The modern pursuit of knowledge, forever and by definition, posits its goal in the future and deposits it in the past. This very idea of the past and of the future as somehow separate realms of existence is itself modern and cannot hold in the face of what we have called, by comparison, contemporary knowledge. For a contemporary human being, world is not out there, as distinct and separate from the self in here, but for him there is world and self in unison. Needless to say, such reality is not open to inspection from a modern point of view. The modern spirit is neither able nor permitted to enter. Those who desire to become contemporary human beings must leave their modernity behind. For many of us what is required here is a radical rethink of fundamental issues. The change-over from modern to contemporary can be turned into a less painful exercise, can even become a joyful venture, with the help of the right sort of education. The only alternative to our taking the reins resolutely in both hands is being run over by the cart.

State education is these days being run over by the cart. How this relates to the nation and to the state is matter for another enquiry. Our present task is to acquaint ourselves with the radical difference between school curriculum as state-educational and school curriculum as creative-educational, because teacher training must make this difference increasingly clear. I say 'increasingly' because it would be nonsensical to suppose that this clarity can be neatly achieved with concepts in an armchair. The person who is to understand what is at stake here will himself be changed. Training is required, and a period of transition during which theory and practice continually dovetail.

We leave to the side any discussion of state-education curriculum for the time being and concentrate mainly on what might be called, without too much risk of distortion or misrepresentation, the curriculum, or even the secondary curriculum, of education as art-work and of education as creativity.

When a teacher trainee has become somewhat adept at his voluntary and good inwardness, to the point, perhaps, where he is able to initiate various faculty responses as solicited by his guide, he may then contemplate such things as outward examples of what he means. Just as contemporary world, or real world, is 'an infinite number' of outward examples of what he in himself amounts to as an individual human being in communality with others, so will his curriculum now exemplify what he perceives as an inward experience of the moment. Again we are in the presence not of a wilful, but of a graceful act. The trainee allows the curricular example to suggest itself to him. He must be willing to be surprised. He knows, because he has learned, that it lies in the nature of parental human experience that such current examples suggest themselves, uniquely apt, in the face of any truly educational effort. Children want to be educated. There is a natural demand, by the child, that should be raised, and the parental adult knows that children must be raised and educated. An organic context exists for all these experiences and activities.

What must be avoided here at all cost is that the trainee should try to present something as an example that he has accepted only on hearsay. Technically he cannot succeed, because in that case it would not be an example of his inwardness but something extinct. Only by remaining alert to his own instinctive inwardness and to the faculties he initiates here can he actually identify and reject any extinct phenomena. Gradually he will learn to discriminate sensitively, between instinct and extinction. This is again an important transition period. The guide now becomes a leader, who leads the trainee out to where more and more relevant examples are entertained, described, explained perhaps too, though explanation is most difficult, since we are far too accustomed to dead-end explanations to come up with one that truly satisfies. The practical use of these exercises is to strengthen the bond between what the trainee knows and what he talks about. Rather than moving into an area of pretension or presumptuousness he should change topic, move from one concern to another, mindful of links between one example and the next. All of his examples must occur to him from his personal outward experience, and so that he does not get carried away he must maintain and re-establish the link with his present personal surroundings, his guide and leader, and his fellow trainees. It is primarily for them and for their benefit that he exercises this exemplary faculty, just as previously he practiced the faculties of vision, of imagination and fantasy, of emotion and thought, etc. This exemplary faculty may be something quite new to him. He may not have any confidence in anything he really knows, only false confidence in extinct information that has been drummed into him. The leader helps him to be less ashamed of what he instinctively knows and more ashamed of the lifeless baggage he carries around with him. Some trainees will gladly return to their childhood, to a time prior to the falsification of their experience. During the training session, they know they are among friends who will not mock them if they offer as a learning example how to tie shoelaces, how to balance across stones over a creek, what an hour in the sun on the meadow with a pet goat means to them. In every case it should somehow be indicated how this experience is an example, and of what, and again the guide must ensure that the cart is not put before the horse and that extinction does not take over.

The guide may, for example, suggest to the trainee something along the line of feeling. The trainee steps forward into a pre-designated part of the room and initiates his faculty of feeling, voluntarily, so that he is able to relate what he feels at that moment as he continues to exercise that faculty. He does not sink back into himself and indulge in psycho-babble, but he might say: "I feel a distinct separation between all of you and me and as I mention it, this isolation disappears. I feel confident standing here at the moment, though somewhat apprehensive about the next stage of this exercise. The room feels warm, a little too warm; my head feels clear. I want to feel happy, and as I mention this, a suitable example occurs to me. Can we brighten our own mood by smiling? The girl I eventually married studied philosophy and we spoke about the power we might have over our mood. Can we voluntarily alter our mood, for example by smiling? This seems to me at this moment to be a good example of how we can, perhaps intentionally, feel one way or another. We smiled at one another. She maintained it made her feel better. I insisted I could tell no difference in myself. I suspect I wanted to contradict her. Perhaps she herself only wanted to prove a point, or to be right." The guide encourages the trainee to develop his thought about the nature of feeling. The trainee continues: "Certainly it seems to me that we should be able to feel as we wish, and that we should not have to wait until we are pushed in some direction by circumstances or events. We can certainly think what we wish. If our feeling is more accidental, usually, this should tell us about ourselves, not about the nature of feeling. We may never have initiated feeling in our life. It must be possible for me to feel sad with those who are sad, and happy with those who are happy. I confess I am not very good at it. Usually I ..." The guide raises his hand. The trainee agrees to stop in mid-sentence. There was danger of enthusiasm leading away from a calm inward connection with the purpose of the exercise. The guide sensitively waits until the trainee has recollected himself. He comments on the aptness of the example as far as it went.

As soon as the guide is of the opinion that the exemplary faculty has been sufficiently exercised in the trainees he prepares for the final stage, when he himself suggests examples of experience, which will coincide only to some extent and degree with personal experience of the trainees. They must all now, in turns, relate as best they can to the guide's suggestion, and what they say should be introduced by the attestation that they know this or else that they have heard it said or have read it without ever having personally experienced it. For example the guide may ask them to accept the phenomenon of electricity. A trainee begins with personal experience. He has seen electric sparks, high tension wires. He has heard the crack of lightning. He associates power points, light bulbs and motors with electricity. Another trainee takes over, always stepping first into the pre-designated space. This trainee has experienced a severe electric shock and he describes this in detail. By now these trainees are aware of the workings of their inwardness and they are able to give visual accounts, to express emotion to make a point more emphatically, they are able to orchestrate their verbal deliveries with patience, drama, gestures, energy as required and they know how to respond to their own insecurities, anxieties, emotions and thoughts as these accidentally crop up. The third trainee relates his experience of having to draw diagrams in school to illustrate the workings of electric magnets without having the least understanding of why these things were said to work the way they did, and he mentions that now for the first time he has admitted this to himself. The guide suggests the horse as another curricular example. Once again all supposition and hearsay is trimmed away from each trainee's personal experience. The trainees are now not any more embarrassed to reveal how little they know. They are not allowed to enthuse or to 'rave' about anything, only to speak articulately and to let their bodies and limbs and face speak along with their voice. No standard is applied. Individual preference is respected.

Finally the realm of hearsay and supposition is tapped, very tentatively at first. The guide suggests light. Molecules, atoms, wave length, speed of light are mentioned. The straight line is discussed, though no one has ever seen one that fits the usual definition. The faculty that is developed here is the hear-say detector. The arctic timber wolf is hearsay to one trainee because he has never seen one. He keeps this in mind as he relates what he knows about it.

Children are harmed by teachers who speak of things as though they had personal knowledge of them, when in fact they have only chosen to accept someone else's opinion.

* * *

28. Teacher Training III

(with reference to education as art)

If we want to speak intelligently of teaching as an art, then we must ask ourselves what we mean by art. Those of us who end up practicing an art, began by having to define for themselves what they would intend to achieve with this activity. To be gifted is one thing. To come up with sufficient character for a genuine piece of work is another. To the public mind an artist is an artist and we like what reminds us of ourselves after a complimentary fashion. There is an art, however, which lays the public mind aside and concentrates on the revelation of the truth. In a sense we are all either popular or human today, depending on whether we strive for the truth or else allow ourselves to be duped by the various appeals to our massive instincts.

It's enough to strive for the truth in order, at that moment, to possess it. The simple human faith we are born with allows us to assert ourselves in accordance with that fact. To be in possession of truth is the same as to wish to reveal it to others. Two strains, two different qualities come to light here, which justify us in making a distinction between art and great art. The distinction is not so much one of judgment as of appreciation. The practitioner of an art that is not great, or not yet great, is not fully aware that to strive for the truth means to be in possession of the truth, so he repeatedly returns to the beginning of his art and starts afresh, almost as if he were under a compulsion to re-invent himself after every work, or after every series of works. Evidence of this is frequently a self-sacrificial bent, or, on the other side of the coin, a callous contempt for 'the ignorant public'.

But we have to be careful here. Public acclaim is no real indication of anything. Great art is sometimes practiced in relative obscurity and comes to light after centuries. Our only sure guide is the regenerate human heart. Here is where all that is to last must begin, where all that is to stand must be erected. From an unregenerate heart great artists may spring forth but they end as dead points of reference within the confines of history.

*

All true art to some extent teaches. If only it encourages us to look up and beyond our narrow vision, this is a teaching. And if it practically enables us to transcend our various lifeless states of being, then this is a great teaching, and the art of which it is a function should be treated by us, for our own sake, with reverence. But alas!

That teaching and education should itself amount to an art, or simply to art, this may well prove, in time, a most beneficial response to the predicament and misery of our time.

Two different approaches can be identified here, among the multiple experiments with education these days. One of these begins from standard, traditional education and hopes to embrace the advantages of art, while the other takes as its starting point the traditional principles of art in the hope of developing from these new and fruitful habits of education. Both of-these can only halfway succeed. In the former case nothing will be achieved to help children out of states of mortification into which they have strayed or been pressed due to neglect or coercive upbringing. Education must, however, be remedial and liberating. Traditional school influence lacks the vision of children as potentially free human beings and substitutes for this vision a picture of children who should become grown-ups adapted to the society of the day. The advantages of art and of creativity can add interest and appeal to this picture, however it remains a visionless scenario all the same. The other approach, from the side of traditional art, must fail for similar reasons. Here one begins with a conception of art as something that serves and services society, with an image of art as play and entertainment, not bound by considerations of ethics and morality. Traditionally the modern artist sees himself only rarely as accountable to the conscience of mankind, for he looks to his public and to its arbiter, the critic. A high goal of modern art over the past twenty centuries has been, and still is today, magical pleasure, today refined subliminally to the point of mass-media charisma. School along such lines is likely to be fun and exciting but the young human being's organic need and subconscious want to be raised to maturity is simply not addressed.

Education as art must therefore be seen as a single impulse that at once responds to the inward and as yet unexpressed desire of children to grow up and mature, and answers the need to be liberated from the mortifying influence due to heredity, society and parental neglect. Such an art cannot rest on principles, nor can rules and standards be prescribed for it. The tradition into which it fits is an unwritten, invisible one, transmitted through the ages by transcendent minds. Its raw materials are the combined individualities of teacher and pupils, its medium is the informed and articulate personality of the teacher and its products, or works, are mature human beings.

It stands to reason that teacher training and development, with the help of which prospective teachers are to become educating and teaching art-workers, must concentrate initially on that adult's individuality where, presumably, the pedagogic germ has begun to sprout.

Art is spontaneity, an overflowing of joyous human being, measured and within recognizable bounds. It is grace and transcendence for the miserable and afflicted. It is sustenance from the realm of reality for those who have not yet arrived there and nourishment for the victims of unfortunate circumstance. Art as true creativity initiates well-being and heals. The living word is a work of art, and so is the alliance of man with man. Human relation and communication are both artful endeavours. Whatever is natural, automatically gives evidence of itself in the shape of art, whether element, mineral, plant, animal or human. Human nature gives artful evidence of itself as human being. If this were universally appreciated, we would all be at home on the earth and not frequently in conflict. So human nature must first be purified, and this too is an effect of mature human art. We know that the living word cleanses us. Then our individuality is ready to bear fruit, each after its own kind.

Prospective teachers must therefore be talented individuals, and as such they will pursue the training of their faculties and the development of their functioning. A talented individual is one who is sure that he wants something but not certain what it is nor in the know of how to go about getting it. Young individuals who are talented are often extremely unhappy because of the depression they experience one day and the high spirits the next. These mood swings frighten them and they feel set apart, isolated from their human environment. This phenomenon has been studied, documented and described from a great variety of angles through the ages, and the consensus seems to be that those who eventually succeed in finding their true vocation or calling have come up with a certain amount of 'stick-to-itiveness' of a primitive kind and most would agree that they have squeezed through a strait gate and that the path was narrow. It must be a great help for such individuals if, during their trials and tribulations, they are cushioned somewhat by a few who know what it means to turn the burden of a talent into a joy. A gifted nature looks first to its environment, hoping to be told: "You are not different. We are like you and we like you." But the gifted nature is different, and not at all liked by those nearby. Why is a gifted nature such a problem among others? Many answers have been given to this, all of a typically modern stamp: He refuses to adjust. The shortage of a certain hormone. A combination of arrogance and cowardice. A burden of heredity. Just plain wickedness, etc. But these are of course all descriptions of the problem and not solutions. The solution requires more than such a dead-end explanation. Transferring a symptom from one sphere of thought to another does not constitute a cure.

A gifted nature is such a problem to others simply because he has not yet sufficiently developed his gifts. What these others reject is something they cannot handle - because the gifted one has not yet learned how to handle it. If among these others there were a few who knew what was going on and who realized what was required, much less talent would be abused and wasted.

A workable ethic does exist for those who would invest their talents and develop their gifts. Another, very much related, ethic is available for those who would be of assistance to them. Perhaps the time has come for adopting this combined ethic in favour and to the specific advantage of those who would develop their gifts in the direction of the education and teaching of the young. The crying need for such a thing has probably never been greater.

Individuals. who wish to invest their talent in the art of teaching, would benefit initially, like all who are gifted, from a thorough acquaintance with what it means to subject oneself to the disciplines that alone can render a gift communicable, and equally with the risks one runs, if talents and gifts are not developed or not properly devolved. A very high and serious sense of moral responsibility needs to be nurtured where any art or creativity is at stake. The generic faculty is not automatically good. We know from experience that wherever the greatest potential for good exists, one also finds the trickiest liability to evil. Genius can go both ways. What is needed is the ability to discern spirits.

To become such a teacher in earnest then means to develop a talent above all conscientiously. Not a social conscience, but a personal conscience is of the essence. Society makes its demands and states its preferences and a creative individual, without disrespecting these, must think and feel for himself. Truth and beauty cannot enter the world via 'the collective'. But neither can they enter via the unregenerate ego. Personal conscientiousness must however be nurtured over a period of time, not with the help of creeds, moral precepts and philosophisticated mumbo- jumbo, but within an atmosphere of compassionate knowledge and understanding.

*

The path from talented individual to creative person can be long and wearying, especially if no common knowledge with respect to it exists. Anyone who would be creative must go through a baptism by fire, there is no getting away from that - unless of course he realizes that he must not if he would. Then progress becomes simpler and easier. It helps to know that others have travelled along this path and arrived at their chosen destination, especially the one who defined the destination in the first place. Once we can accept that he is the path, we can once and for all sacrifice all sacrifice because we know that we have a merciful father. Any attempt to make of sacrifice a standard ethical option then, must seem just a bit silly. If we can have it all, why should we make do with scraps?

The art we mean here, which a teacher is to practice, is not of the sort that would quarrel with science. Only the extinct arts and sciences are somehow at loggerheads, and it cannot be otherwise, because both begin from inside or outside the human being, where the scientist or artist himself does not seem to exist. The live arts and sciences - or let us rather say: live art and science - including philosophy and history, all spring from the same root, which is human spirit, and arrives at the same conclusion, which is communal life on earth in the light of day, for men, women and children.

However, as soon as a disingenuous spirit moves in, this wisdom would much rather not be called anything else at all. Its secret home is the human breast, where the father of all human beings, who is merciful love, lives and works. In here too we find the strength to invest our talents and gifts for one another out here. Everything lies ready for us, we only need to learn how to ask. Teachers who know this may find themselves in a class of their own.

* * *

29. The Blessed Child

There is such a thing as an orderly soul, and where children have that, we stand back and admire them. They seem not like premature adults but like human beings for whom youth is a blessing and not a curse. When we look at them we begin to wonder what it might mean to be young. There is an openness to formative influence; one gets the impression that such children are willing to inspect the world and to look at it from many angles, that they are none to eager to make up their minds and pass judgment, emotionally or mentally. They are blessed with an inner security that allows them to be orderly without being pedantic, well-behaved without being 'good'. They have curiosity and argument, but little need to couple these with insolence and rebellion. Above all, it seems, they have what it takes to remain calm and collected while the elements of vulgarity and dissipation pile up around them.

There is also such a thing as a lively spirit, and where children have that we become cheerful in their company, because the liveliness of youth is infectious to an extent that cannot be traced by reason. An inventive mind, irrepressible good humour, a glad willingness to entertain and be entertained - these are qualities that testify to an enviable inner freedom from anxiety and perhaps to a strength that can cope with anxiety and turn it to good use. If we ourselves could do that, we would be young again, we feel, so we set ourselves to examining our various adult preconceptions, in case one or two of them prevent such a lively spirit from moving into us and lifting us outside ourselves once and again, into one another.

There is also such a thing as healthy flesh, and where children have that we congratulate them and wish them well, because we know that the corruption of the flesh is not at all a necessity, but where we come into conflict we try to make the best of it. Such children have the bloom of youth upon their faces and limbs and they cannot imagine why illness was invented, why teeth should rot, hair fall out and joints get stiff. Theirs is the joy of supreme forgetfulness as they learn how to remember, and their time is an easy one, continuous with the time of plants and animals, of earth and sky. If we envy them we have proof that our attitude towards the flesh is wrong, perhaps morbid and twisted by a preoccupation with empty traditions. We learn from such children that our being male or female is not an accident but an asset, and that often we set ourselves and one another limitations when in our nature they exist ready made.

Flesh, soul and spirit, are all with us present in youth, healthy, lively and orderly, and then, once we are grown up, among the children in our vicinity we detect once again, here and there, clear examples of these, and then we say either: yes, that's how it was, or: yes, that is the beginning. Such children seem to need nothing except to be left alone. They were born with a perfection in one department and one cannot imagine why they should ever be educated or brought up. They can teach us adults more, we feel, than we can teach them. And yet they come to us, with their gracious manner and that direct look in their eyes that makes us suspect a judgment where there is none, and they empty us of all inhibition, of all worry about being mistaken or misunderstood, and for a fraction of an hour we converse with them, almost as if we were conversing with someone we had known intimately for years.

There are not very many such children, but from them we can learn something that we can learn nowhere else and from no one else, and I write what I write here because this is so. We can learn from these children an almost effortless approach to our own human individuality. Is that not a great thing? I wish I could demonstrate how great it really is. To most human beings their individuality is a closed book. They suppose quite wrongly that individuality has something to do with being different and having a right to it. Well, that tells us they are modern, and perhaps even proud to be modern.

But true individuality is our capacity to dissolve inwardly and join with another. How absurd that must sound to the modern individual! And yet a contemporary human being values this ability to be inwardly divisible more highly than any integrity based on principles or beliefs. What keeps you and me separate when we meet, so

200

that we have to draw to our aid artificial conventions if we are not to be appalled by the endless distance between us, is the cruelties we have perpetrated in the past, the meannesses we have instigated, the stupidities we have committed and above all the habitual bad faith. All these form a barrier, or an abyss, between us, and suddenly, in the company of such a blessed child as we have described, that barrier for the fraction of an hour does not exist. We catch a glimpse of what might be. Only adults can build up such barriers, from the authority of their adult will. Children are incapable of it. And most children will find their own circuitous route to a taste of perfection, in spite of what passes for parental guidance in our age.

But look, here we have among us beings who are expressly created to show us how to ease ourselves out of that self-imposed dereliction of spirit, how to move quickly away from the rash habits of our wounded soul, how to settle into our flesh and experience it as benediction. We have these beings among us providentially. They are children, and though they are in the possession of a germinal perfection, it is not enough that we leave them alone, because they too need adult help if they are to mature and not just to become adults. What can we give them that they cannot get for themselves? We may be adults, but perhaps we have not yet a single perfection.

Because we are adults, though we may not be mature, we can put our adulthood at their service and say to them: We two are equal.

You might say that we put our adulthood on the line. For the sake of maturity, equally our own and that child's, we submit our adulthood. Remember that we have nothing to do with becoming adults, only with becoming mature. Our maturity is our responsibility, not our adulthood. We can therefore submit, offer up, or lay down, our adulthood, for a greater cause. Think what this means: "He who gives a glass of water to one of these little ones ..."

You say to such a blessed child: "I do not let my adulthood get in the way between you and me, but for your sake and mine I become your equal. What I myself gain from this is the sort of mature inward contact with reality with which you are gifted, in spirit, in soul or in flesh, and what you gain is awareness in freedom of what this blessing of yours really means and how you can work with it."

We have happened upon a secret here, to do with the educational approach to gifted or blessed children. I do not say talented, because talent describes not a perfection of being but a facility for doing, which in itself is neither good nor bad and must first be harnessed to the good. We distinguish therefore between talented and blessed children. And we take careful note of what it means 'to dissolve our individuality', or 'to submit our adulthood' under certain circumstances. The secret resides in that.

* * *

30. The Cry for Text

Nowadays all that a teacher has to do is follow the guidelines of the department of education and he will know what to teach. He is told there in detail. "The child is to acquire a familiarity with ..." – with one thing or another, such as for example his environment. "Environmental Studies" may be part of the state curriculum. Anyone who uses language sensibly will right away wonder at the amusing difference between studies of the environment and 'environmental studies', but that by the by. A familiarity with our environment can be gained in several ways, but since we take issue with the difference between standard education and creative education we remind ourselves at the outset of the following: standard education imparts the data of its subject-matter to its pupils and then tests the pupils to find out if they have got it, and how much of it. Creative education employs topics of conversation in order to develop the pupils' individuality towards maturity. It would hardly seem fair to apply a common term to the thing that is to enlist the interest of the pupils in both cases. It would not even be true to say that in both cases the interest of the pupils is enlisted. The standard teacher often cannot afford to wait until his pupils are interested because he has to 'cover the ground' during a given period of time. The creative teacher, by comparison, is out to enlist not the interest, but the individuality of his pupils.

Perhaps we should ask why it is that a teacher needs a text book. What use does he intend to make of it? Would he be ignorant without it? Is he lost without it? Does it serve him as a guideline, as a crutch, or as personal inspiration? Perhaps he only now and again needs his memory jogged. Does it make him nervous to sit in font of his pupils when he has nothing to talk about? Would anything at all do, just so long as those pupils do not begin to behave awkwardly, out of sheer boredom with having nothing presented to them to occupy their minds?

The fact that children have to be educated whether they like it or not has to be balanced against the truth that children want to be raised, that they want to grow up. If these two do not match, to that extent there is trouble.

Can we imagine a text book for a creative teacher? What would it look like? If he intends to talk about 'the environment', does he mean the children's environment or the environmental scientist's environment (what is a scientist when he is environmental?), or perhaps the teacher's environment? Remember that the scientist will talk about environment in abstraction. In a text book he would present a world view of something called 'the environment'. As soon as a child hears about 'the environment' his gaze is taken away from his own personal environment and fastened to a set of abstractions agreed upon, for the time being, by a set of individuals who have decided to make an issue of it. This set of abstractions, 'environmental studies', is something most peculiar because it exists nowhere in particular but only in some people's minds. The creative teacher has no use for it because he wishes to present to his pupils only such entities as they can themselves relate to and inspect because they exist in reality, as infinite entities, open to a multitude of approaches and patient of personal enquiry. Any cut and dried formula for how to look at what goes on around him is anathema to him. His own environment is different from that of his pupils in that he brings to it an adult and mature point of view. The maturity is what his pupils are after, not a number of pigeon holes for sorting dead facts.

So any creative teacher could certainly make a point of drawing the attention of his pupils to how he, their teacher, views his surroundings, maturely and with a fresh eye, not prejudicially but generously, not morbidly but soberly expectant of wonder, and so on. Really the only text book one can imagine here is one written by the teacher himself as he shapes his environment in exemplary fashion. The only use such a book would be to another teacher is as an example of how an individual point of view can be communicated, or personalized. But that other teacher, though he might be inspired by this book, would still have to discover his own link to his environment before he could be useful to his pupils, because precisely such a discovery is mature, and creative, not the repetition of someone else's discovery. And his maturity, not facts, information and data, is a creative teacher's pedagogic medium.

If we ask ourselves finally what sort of a text would be of benefit to a teacher whose chief aim is the maturity of his pupils, we are put in mind of the classics scholar, whose endless notes on diversely related topics were eventually to add up to a textbook on ancient Rome and Greece. He married a young wife, who burnt the lot because she wanted him to attend more to her, which he did then, though in a fashion so peculiar that soon she regretted her action and fled to her parents. "The man has no sense of perspective," she complained. "He can only deal with what he sees in front of him if he imagines it turned into a lifeless object. There is no helping him. His cry is forever for instant gratification of his intellect. I will have none of him" Eventually she learned to do without male companionship altogether. But here the story ceases to interest us. We hear that cry for instant gratification of the intellect echoing through the modern age and we know what it means. The senses have been sacrificed. Life has become a textbook. One keeps it handy to fall back on. The merit of an experience is judged by its proximity to text and by its transformability into it. Meanwhile the human body is a corpse.

* * *

31. The fundamental disposition of gratitude

As we set out to do anything here during the course of a day, we are perhaps driven to it, by ourselves or circumstances, or we do it reluctantly, because we would much rather do something else or nothing. Out of necessity death is our taskmaster, because, while we live, we suppose we might readily die.

And yet there is nothing in death itself that injures or harms us. We fend for ourselves until we are guided by wisdom to fend for some others. How readily death disappears in the background then.

Pain has its moments. Outwardly pain is a vivid preventative, a guiding principle. We leave ourselves open to less of it than would appear. Inwardly pain is so downright scandalous that we drag ourselves out of its reach at any cost.

But the man who has learned to suffer seems to have less pain than most. How can this be? We can only imagine that suffering uses pain up. This is unusual. Those who avoid pain are stiff and crabbed, and behold, they are hollow. How does it come that we make such a mess of our lives when we chase the next comfort, the next happy sensation, and when we live for the holiday, the paradise beyond, while the man who gladly suffers what comes to him is nourished as though he were a child?

Are children more grateful? Do children step out into rain or sunshine and make no demands that their lot should be different? At least we may say that a child takes for granted the earth beneath his feet, the sky above his head. The younger child has the finer connection to the elements of the universe. So there we may look for what it means to be grateful.

*

The young child is grateful but never for this or for that. That is why parents do well to reflect before they insist that their offspring say 'thank you'. Imagine if someone made you say 'tree' every time you bump into a tree but made you say nothing when you come up against a wall, a horse or a bicycle. You would wonder what it was about trees. To very young children everything is given, whether out of the hand of a person or not. They are glad they are able to receive. The very light of day they accept with a matter of fact demeanour that implies all the same that a treasure is being laid up and that something is being possessed. There is no insecurity about supply, and when something is withdrawn, such as the daylight when night sets in, then this too is accepted.

*

So from very young children we can learn the art of accepting what is given. Do children ever do this ungratefully? It's inconceivable. Telling a child to say thank you is therefore really superfluous, is an empty social gesture, unless - unless that child has in the meanwhile been infected by greed. Greed is not accepting at all. Greed is taking. And greed is not taking for the sake of having but it is taking for the sensation of taking. What a remarkable thing is greed! How pointless, really. And yet, who would cast the first stone – ?

Once greed has come into the world of the child, and once the child has tasted the pointless sensation of taking for the sake of taking, then and only then, and reminiscent of the time when all was given and accepted out of hand, does gratitude come into the picture, more or less as a corrective. We dimly do ourselves recall what it once was like when the world was there for us and before we became anxious that it might not be there unless first we take it and keep it from others.

However, not only, and not even mainly, as a corrective do we now bring gratitude into the picture. We cannot return to the place where we were. A new place has been made ready for us, where we once again accept, just as we did then, this is true, but in addition we know what it is we accept, and we know who we are who are doing the accepting. We have matured and this knowledge is our birthright. And this knowledge is tantamount to life!

As the gratitude, that is first brought into our existence as a corrective and as a stimulus to awareness after greed and ingratitude have had their dulling and stupefying effect, eventually leavens our entire approach to one another and the world, we give and forgive in a spirit of generosity and largesse. Our sharing, transferring and exchanging must be done at least gratefully if we are to benefit, else what we have is taken from us, and frequently our life.

If once we have overcome that tenacious and sensual tendency to greed in ourselves, in our spirit, our soul and our flesh, we soon enough become aware that we have just as much reason to be grateful for the inconvenient as for the convenient, for the unpleasant as for the pleasant, for the setback as for the furtherance. For pain, though it is partially a sign that we are worthy of being corrected, it is more chiefly the uncomely messenger of good news and bringer of gifts, if we but approach it gratefully with that thought in mind. So gratitude in that sense is the key to unlock doors we ourselves have closed against life and happiness.

Not a great deal of greediness needs to enter a child's life before education can avail itself of that opportunity to bring a conscious gratitude to bear. But it must be kept in mind that gratitude is originally a human natural way to be for a child, in the sense that younger children are not naturally greedy or ungrateful. Where greed is detected in a child, the mature parental adult has a golden opportunity for more life if he now extends gratitude and generosity, consciously and intentionally, towards that child - and the child gains real knowledge. You can imagine what it means to a child to be freed from such a handicap as greed, for greed poisons us sexually, psychically and supernaturally, so that our concourse with one another and the world becomes a mere shadow-play.

* * *

32. The Good Child

No man can be good. Can children be good? A lot of damage has been done by telling children to be good. It's not just a matter of semantics. It's adults who suppose they themselves might be good who tell children to be good - and usually with that special emphasis: "I'll make you be good, because I can't manage it myself." So telling children to be good, either in so many words or by a thousand implications, is a form of criticism, and criticism is an illness in the event of spreading.

Churches are established in the supposition that people can be good – if they do what they're told, and those who tell them are the very ones who should know better, because what they call being good is so often based on the absence, not on the overcoming, of the bad. If we fit into a club of people who are all good because they belong to that club and fit into it noticeably, we are very likely to demand or cajole that our children should be good. But no man or woman can be good. So how can we ask this of children?

"Can I have a bicycle for Christmas, Mummy?" - "Only if you're good!"

Oh alright, so that means nothing more than: "Only if you don't annoy me, only if you do as you're told." Is that all it means? But that's quite a lot. If my child annoys me, does that automatically mean he is at fault and not I? If he doesn't do as he is told, how about taking a quick look at who is doing the telling and why he is doing it.

So in that more innocent sense, "Be good!" usually means: "Don't grow, don't change, that is to say: be dead. I myself am dead and I resent these signs of life in you. Here I have a program laid out for your next hour, your day, your whole life, and instead of thanking me and mutely pulling that load up the hill you kick over the traces. For shame! You are not good. No bicycle for Christmas."

Of course it's important for children to learn how to obey genuine authority - if there is any. Genuine authority pulls its own weight, has no use for force. Obedience is gradually solicited by authority. Being obedient has nothing to do with being good.

The good child does not exist, but has figured out how to sneak past the foibles of adults by faking it. Babies are good when they don't scream much; when they sleep all the time they are really good. As children get older they soon learn what it means to be good and they either fake it or they don't. If they don't fake it they are scolded for being bad. Some of them then give their conscience a jolt, because they hate to be nagged at, and bribed, and punished for all those accidents when they momentarily slip into spontaneous behaviour. They go against their conscience, which is not so difficult because it only just got started. Without a conscience they can much more successfully be good. They do this not as an adult might, scheming and calculating, but more or less in a daydream. They are capable of many successive small adjustments inwardly, which allow them to get on, among those who want them to be good, much less painfully. For a child such a compromise, when the budding moral awareness is sacrificed for being good to please the adults, is not so much an act of wickedness as a primitive survival tactic. Talking to such good children, if one appeals to the whole personality, can turn into a problem, because what you say to them must seem to them irrelevant. You are asking them to mature but they have geared themselves to being good, and the two cannot match. The crux of the irreconcilable difference can easily and quite informatively be discussed in terms of conscience.

What is it that makes a child aware for the first time of his inward being? Probably a pain. Then a great deal depends on how he copes with this pain. If his greatest inward pain is due to the displeasure of adults who chide him for not being good and who reward him for being good then he can deal with that pain by repeatedly denying his inward being. If you punish a child for being bad rather than good you point out to him, painfully, his inward being and at the same time you make it impossible for him to develop his inward being, to grow inwardly, since being good is a fake constraint, so he has the choice to either rebel against you or to rebel against himself. If he rebels against you, he will probably end up with even more pain, but if he rebels against himself he will deny his inward being so that in future he should become insensitive and invulnerable. At liberty from his inward being he can then be good too, by automatically falling in with your plans for him. You are getting him ready for a mechanistic existence, by rewarding him for being good and punishing him for being not good. If you punish him for repeatedly tracking dirt onto your carpet or for torturing the cat he will experience an inward pain too, but right away now he should also have a notion of cleanliness and kindliness. Consequently his inward being is being presented with the freedom to grow. He can be more careful next time, and more considerate, and that will play into various aspects of his behaviour.

If you hurt a child because he isn't good, what you are doing is not punishment at all but vengeful. And by hurting a child I mean also such behaviour as withdrawing your affection and replacing it with indifference or criticism. If, however, you punish a child, you are not meddling with his being but influencing his functioning, which is what he does or does not do.

And, by the same token, giving a child pleasure because he 'is good' is not rewarding him at all but a bribe. A reward must again fall in line with something he has done, not with how he was. And you bribe the child most successfully, of course, by piling on your affection and your sentimentality in the absence of all discernment.

It's a great pity when children pretend to be good and parents or teachers approve of this, or when adults want children or pupils to be good. The human being of the child is arrested in its development and the outcome is a kind of ritualized adult behaviour, where good people keep track of other good people so that no one should give the game away. If such people follow a Religion, they usually manufacture for themselves a God after their own image and surround him with a multitude of taboos.

If children are taught - and shown - that only god is good, then they have the freedom to learn how to be human, which is tricky enough under any circumstances. And then, being human, they can learn how to <u>do</u> good, and this is an activity that holds out exciting prospects for any human being. The more good we do the more human we become. Meanwhile good people turn into do-gooders, who, to all intents and purposes, are definitely a breed apart.

Of course there are those who say: If a child cannot be good he must be bad. But children, like grown-ups, only become bad by doing bad, and by not doing good.

* * *

33. The Killing of the Sensitivity for Life

There is such a thing as a sensitivity for life and very few have it. Those who have it again can usually recall that once they had it but then they lost it. While they were without it they didn't realize they were without it because during that time they were attached to dead sensations. They had come to believe that the only choice was between dead sensations and nothing. On one side boredom, despair, indifference and on the other side a cheap thrill, vicarious experience and a promise of ecstasy. On one side pointless duties, a repetitive job, empty relationships and on the other side a little pleasure, periodic anaesthesia, another affair.

Given that choice, who would hesitate? Children who are neither brought up nor educated, cynically observe the hopelessly immature adults in their vicinity and invariably come to the one conclusion: "If that's what it means to grow up, I don't want it. Give me then those harmless little pleasures, so that I may break down and burn out as quickly as possible. This adolescent anger, this adolescent rage - is a bind, is a hang-up. Plenty of energy, nothing to do with it, consequently moral exhaustion, an interest in crime, in anything illicit or illegal - give me instead the narcotic; at least I won't notice what a mess I'm in."

Let those who speak of drug abuse reflect: how many other abuses preceded? Before a teenager is tempted to experiment with mind-bending and body-enriching drugs he must be in a state where reality does not exactly interest or reward him. Now reality is a marvel and a stimulant to growth. What has happened to our senses that we cannot take that in? The world is an exquisite creation, revealed to all who have eyes and ears. Does anyone seriously not believe that? What has happened to our capacity for creative belief? Who is it can get through a day and say at the end: "Now that was worthwhile!" Whenever we cannot say that, something was wrong with how we lived that day. Perhaps we were only half awake, only one quarter in touch. Maybe we barely took an interest. Are we really convinced that life is worth living? Then why can we not pass that conviction on to our children? Do we expect them to nod comprehensively when we tell them it's a tough world, it's a hard grind, neither fair nor rewarding, and it's dog eat dog, a rat race, and if you don't perform some meaningless job for a hundred pounds a fortnight you'll only get ninety-five on the dole, for shame! Best of all, strap yourself into a career, because that produces adrenalin.

"So does a jog around the park," says the teenager. He will not be fooled by adults. If he is going to be fooled he will choose his own way. If a joint can make the world look rosy then a joint is the thing. The treadmill lies ahead, youth has been sacrificed; the front door to the kingdom is traditionally bolted, so let's sneak in through the back. Of course we will get kicked out but we can always try again. And again. Until we're addicted to trial. Until we become a thorough trial to all those who are responsible for our up-bringing. It's a way of getting our own back – not that we think much of it.

So before we rush to join the chorus of anti-drug abusers, let's ask ourselves: Are we sensitive to life? How do we behave when boredom sets in? How do we deal with disappointment, with loss, with the next person who sleights or insults us? If we look forward to anything tomorrow, has it anything to do with beauty, with honour, with joy? Could we walk up to the next adolescent and with hand on heart say: "Grow up, like myself, because its great!" Sure we are never done lying to ourselves, and to one another, about what makes existence desirable. Once the animal spirits are exhausted, what have we left? There is alcohol, nicotine and the television. There is sex and the next great sensation. There is an abundance of pseudo-philosophies, all dedicated to help us get rid of our pain and ignore our problems so that we can get on, energetically and feeling good, with our usual trivial business. There are artificial stimulants and depressants for the body, the mind and the soul, for the spirit and the flesh. They come in a great variety of shapes and sizes and most of them are sanctioned by tradition, by a cultural hierarchy, by our peers, or just plain by our own egotistical preference. Self-enhancement – how often every day do we inject ourselves with that? How often do we stick our face into that plastic bag that smells so deliciously of popular acclaim? Or we inebriate ourselves with another man's elaborate thought system because we cannot be bothered to think for ourselves - and the police cannot bust us. Truly we are wonderful examples to our offspring! I think what disgusts us most is that they insist on their own delusions. We resent their inventiveness when it comes to lying. Once a soulless, materialistic existence has become the norm, we would like our children to abide by it, and not branch out into wanton spirituality. If you must turn into a vegetable, kindly do it on a decent income in front of a television set while swirling a brandy. Or keep it under control. A joint now and again, what's wrong with that? The reason I can stop there is because I am half dead in any case. It takes passion and energy to get properly hooked, stop being so young! – Wonderful arguments!

Reality, thank god, is a perpetual challenge. The only way to avoid that frequently painful challenge is to turn into something other than a human being - which means, into something less than a human being. Human beings are endowed with a desire for eternal life and there is no getting around that. We have that in us from birth. As young children we enjoy the foretaste of it. We are 'in life'. Then gradually, if things go well, we learn to live. We need those parental adults around us to show us how to do it, to spur us on, to set us personal examples. Then maturity comes along and lo and behold! - we have life. We can grasp it, touch it and taste it. We embrace it. With maturity we have arrived. We have eternal life. How do we keep it? We give it to others, to those who still need it. How do we increase it? We diminish it for one another, we serve one another.

As we begin to learn how to live, around the age of five or six - if all goes well - there is something that develops in us ever so gradually. Our parental companions, parents and teachers, look for it and cherish it. And if they don't, they should. What is it?

The sense of life. But by life we don't mean the animal spirits, or triumphant survival. By life we don't mean the psyche oiled by ideological dogma or public acclaim. By life we mean eternal life.

The corruption of our sense of life, and of our sensitivity to life, is the most reprehensible act imaginable. The one single goal every educator sets himself, if he is an educator indeed, perhaps as a poet, as a philosopher or a teacher in a classroom, is the rescue and development of that organ, because without it no other sense can really

217

thrive. Emotion substantiates it. Feeling supports it. Then it is turned towards the world and other human beings in it.

If we set ourselves this goal, as parental adults who have the true welfare of the children in their vicinity at heart, we will undertake to create conditions under which this sense will thrive; we will take pains to devise means by which this sense, this way of seeing and knowing and understanding the world and human beings, is eventually brought to the attention of children, so that they can truly mature. We may, for example, send our children to a creative school, where they are not measured and minted in accordance with the times but encouraged to develop as individual human beings. And then we entertain the hope that they might be able to withstand at least the worst abuses of the age.

One of the worst abuses of our age is the mass media. What we have here is a medium that is itself abusive. The foremost representative of this medium is television; there's at least one set in nearly every home, and usually in the living-room. And the best way of preventing a house from turning into a home is to infect it with a television set. That foreign body will succeed where other means, such as greed for material possessions, irreligion, immorality and lack of trust only make a partial go of it.

It's difficult to express what it is, exactly, about this medium that makes it so invidious. The mass media lay claim to our attentiveness in a way that is neither passive nor active but magical. And magic is effective - or affective - in two directions. On one side it pacifies, stupefies and drugs, so that any brutish instincts, any raw animal energies in us are for the time being put out of action, in the sense that they are doped. This is the narcotic effect of magic, the opium that people prefer when the only alternative they see is cutting one another's throats or jumping in front of a bus. And the other effect of magic, and of the mass media, and in particular of television, is that it prevents the real other alternative from coming to the fore. So magic positively justifies its existence by covering up reality and by spoiling our good appetite for reality. That's why we come to depend on it. It's all the same whether we watch a wildlife program or Neighbours, whether Bruckner's fourth symphony or the latest rock group massages our soul.

All human beings are creative in some way, and that implies, among other things, that raw energy is welcome and fed carefully into some creative process so that good action results. A human being resents having his raw-materials messed with. When he makes a mistake he learns from it and doesn't right away throw out the baby with the bathwater.

Television, then, to pick out only one of the many mass media available today, strikes at the very root of creativity, so that rot sets in. It's absolutely amazing to see so-called institutions of education employing mass media to aid the education process. In that way our children are literally dehumanized. We pride ourselves on our twentieth century enlightenment because of the various superstitions we have allegedly put behind us, but an addiction to magic is worse than superstition. That parents should send their children to a creative school and at the same time subject them to mass media influence at home is a sign that there is room for improved insight.

And then of course arrives the perfectly understandable craving, in those children, for injecting a bit of glamour into their dullened existence. First the sensitivity is destroyed, by mass media indulgence, and then the artificial kick, the chemical boost is necessary, for a semblance of vitality. Of course it's only a semblance, we know it's a lie, but surely that's no great shame where the truth is covered over in any case?

So first comes the mass media culture. The drug user's scene is a reaction to it.

*

So that certain special sensitivity to what truly moves us, to what is really and truly good for us to experience and to do, has to be something we have heard of, at least, before we can reasonably judge between what nourishes it and what harms it. Otherwise we are bound to say: "What's all this about? What's the big fuss about mass media, about television, walkmans and computer games? It's a phase. After that it will be something else. As long as you don't overdo it. There are good programs on television. And it's educational ...etc., etc."

A creative educator knows about this human sensibility, she is familiar with it and she possesses it, so she is never done devising ways and means for breaking through the pupil's habitual dullness of spirit, for counteracting the pupil's acquired taste for magical rubbish, for arousing the pupil's human natural appetite for the rich reality available both within and without him. If parents refuse to co-operate with the teacher, her task becomes nearly impossible, because whatever is built up at school is undone at home. The most she can do then is

220

point out a direction and for the rest resign herself to a few happy coincidences.

The sensitivity for real life is perhaps dead in many grown-ups in any case and from them we cannot expect any initiative until something from outside them forces them to reconsider. But in young children that sense is ready to come into being and to develop, and woe to those who harm one of these little ones. It's not so bad while we do it in ignorance, but once we know, and then we neglect or abuse, there is no excuse. Our willingness to be implicated in the daily destruction of this sensitivity, without which neither real joy nor useful suffering is possible, would astonish us if we knew better. But the measure of our success in life is always our willingness to learn, even if it hurts our precious self-esteem - or perhaps especially then.

* * *

34. The Religious Child

Young children are not by definition bored, unruly and unresponsive to affection. Something has to be done to them to make them lose interest, to disappoint them. They have to be neglected in various ways if they are to lose touch with their own inner friendliness and their readiness to trust. Creative education not only appeals to the child's natural wish to grow up but also identifies the various fruits of abuse and neglect at any given time and place and then hinges the maturation of the child to the overcoming of these shortcomings.

In very young children the trust, or 'belief', as we might call it, is very nearly complete. Injuries are readily forgiven, there is almost no will to hit back. Perhaps we can recall from our own early childhood how we seemed quite at home in ourselves. Pain jarred our system, we swung back into a dream and were healed. Not much was in doubt. What we thought was barely distinct from what we felt and what we desired lay close to what we wanted. It seems almost inappropriate to describe childhood in adult language, and when someone speaks of "these little ones, whose angels forever face their father", that seems as apt a description as any, of the inner connectedness of children, of their being in touch with the very essence of their being, with their humanity.

Now we can take it for granted that children organically 'want' to grow up; and we, as adults, would certainly like them to be mature, because we ourselves are mature and because we think very highly of maturity and of all that it entails, such as for example the ability to consciously and intentionally love, especially when we don't feel like it. As parental adults, such as parents, teachers, or anyone who wishes children well and would like to do them some good, we cannot imagine why children should ever lose that essential belief or trust. Some say this is necessary so that something else can take its place. But perhaps we feel tempted to assume it must happen because it so nearly always does happen. We have among us a few ten-year-olds who are so trusting that we fear for their safety in society; it seems simpler to label such children as backward than to take society to task.

Two facts must be accepted by us as true: If once we have lost the essential belief and trust of our childhood, we can regain it, and – there is no reason for this trusting belief ever to be lost.

As educators we are aware of what makes the difference between trust maintained and trust regained. Injury, pain and waste make the difference. If we were to insist on the most apt use of the word religion we would use it to describe what goes on and what is achieved, in terms of love and by loving, as we regain, again and again, our essential believing trust. There is something in 'religion' that implies a bond or connection re-established. And we have it from good authority that love does this best. No one can really help another human being, child or adult, if human love is missing. Without that we go through the motions of self-delusion.

*

In the light of this notion of religion as re-bonding with god and fellow man, what could it mean to speak of a religious child? Well, mainly, I suppose, it means, that, considering the make-up of a child, the repair, or the re-bonding, after a disruption, happens quite readily, almost as if it were being done for the child. We can think of this as an organic resilience. In spite of the fact that most adults around most children have forgotten or mislaid their own childhood, so that they see children only as imperfect adults, for which imperfection they need to be punished, tolerated and schooled – in spite of this kind of treatment many children hang on surprisingly long to their inborn and instinctive conviction that things will be somehow alright. I think of this as a kind of religious tenacity. It makes sense only if we imagine that children must be in fairly good hands, by and large, in spite of some of the so-called up-bringing and education they undergo. It takes long years of subtle cruelty and love-deprivation to pervert the religious instinct of a child.

223

The creative educator comes along and says: Let's turn this religious instinct into an instinct for religion. If children are not human-naturally suspicious, divisive and malicious, and if they do have this knack for staying in touch and getting in touch again with human reality, or "with their father in heaven", then let's do all we can so that this should not be perverted but that it should develop. As adults we value nothing more than our ability really and truly to communicate. We love to get together and we get together to love, because we know how wisdom, achievement and growth make their home here. Considering that such communality is like the life breath of a child, we must do our best now to make sure that the adult version of it actually does come about.

And the adult version of the religious instinct is really and truly an instinct for religion. Up-bringing and education are required to take us from one to the other; it won't happen absent-mindedly. If children are not brought up and educated they turn into adults alright, but into immature adults. When you mention immaturity to an educator he becomes alert, his fingers itch and he rolls up his sleeves.

From religious instinct to instinct for religion is a metamorphosis; that word describes it best. The classic image is still the change from caterpillar through pupa to butterfly. The insect as larva goes through the chrysalis stage before it unfolds, as imago. This unfolding is maturity, and it's a wonderful event. I wonder how many adults have experienced it. I never tire of searching for those who have, because they are the ones we need for bringing up and educating children. Adults who have never tasted maturity, or who rush into every opportunity for falling, if not climbing, into immaturity, know nothing of the instinct for religion and they can do the religious child no good. They may be the most respected Christians or the most turned-on Buddhists on god's little acre, but I say: keep them away from children.

The instinct for religion displayed by a mature adult in the company of children cannot take on a predetermined form. This is a bitter pill to swallow for those of us who like agendas, programs and plans. Where the metamorphosis of human beings is concerned, specifically, there an educator or teacher must remain, and become again, painstakingly flexible. He observes how he tends to harden into ritual, custom and routine, and he makes it his primary responsibility to counteract that tendency. He notices how every truly successful move he makes in his capacity as teacher within this realm of religious development and evolution begins in one form and ends in another. He cannot contain his pedagogic approach within a single, predictable format and be effective.

His own instinct for religion, however, will inform him reliably as to what moves to make and how to make them. He knows how to rely on his inward resources for trusting and believing and he knows how to behave and express himself in the light of this. And he realizes that he is not after all operating in a vacuum, but with children, who bring with them their own best resources and who are generally much in favour of linking up with someone who can 'unfold'.

* * *

35. The teacher of religion

Let's get away from speaking of 'the' teacher, and let's instead consider teachers of religion, because we are not concerned with ideals here but with practicalities. I would like you to tell me how to prepare myself for teaching religion. The first thing you ask me is: How do you deal with your setbacks?

I think I know why you start with that. You want to know whether I can see the growth-potential in a disappointment. Then, when I tell you that I can, you will probably ask whether I usually behave in accordance with that insight. You will inquire about my integrity. Do I say, but not do. Am I a hypocrite who preaches without practicing. Do I make promises I don't hold.

Then you will probably want to know whether I wait until I am pushed into a corner and stuck there before I apply some of my good sense or am I able to take advantage of good fortune and build on it. I am glad you asked those questions, because they encourage me to think about a lot of things that I have pushed to the back of my mind, and even further away, to the bottom of my soul.

I would reply to your questions in the following manner. The first point, to my way of thinking, comes down to courage. When I suffer a set-back, when my plans are overturned, when I have to cease functioning for a time, I first of all resent that and it frightens me. I am not being honest if I don't admit that to you. It happens to me automatically that I try to lay blame, to accuse and hit back. But then it occurs to me that I am on the wrong track and that I should be looking for the benefit that has just been conferred on me. That used to sound like a contradiction to me but today I see in it the perfect consequence. What has helped me see that truth, is my behaviour on numerous occasions when I acted in accordance with it, during times of frustration and defeat, especially during an illness, I might add, but also when my grandiose plans did not pan out. But what has helped me keep that truth in mind is my concentrated application to it, in one way or another, at times when everything was going well, when I was in high spirits, happy, content with myself. When I sat down then and said: "If I don't now invest all this pleasant and convenient life in a creative work I will lose it all," and then I did a creative work - then something positive and substantial sank into me permanently, though it might have been weeks before I knew the benefit of it and could actually draw on it, spontaneously, as on a resource.

This is to let you know that I am well aware of the sort of thing you are talking about when you mention the ability to discover the plenty in every shortcoming, the strength in every weakness, the health in every sickness, the thing I called courage; and when you mention truthfulness and integrity.

I agree with you that a teacher of religion must be well versed in this business of everyday renewal. That's what is supposed to be going on with all of us, really, all the time, and it should be part and parcel of what we ordinarily call living. We are constantly surrounded, inwardly and outwardly, believe it or not, by live influences after the order of renewal but because of our ignorance, our bad faith, our arrogance and cowardice, we get ourselves into states where these renewal influences are bound to appear inconvenient and unpleasant, painful and

227

ugly. All the same, these nuisances are messengers of glad tidings. It's up to us to interpret them - religiously. I think that's a fair application of the word.

But shouldn't a teacher of religion be able to talk about god? Or about God?

I really don't think so. Not nowadays. We have to take account of the times we live in, and of the fact that certain topics have been so talked into extinction, and twisted out of all recognition, and abused beyond the point of endurance, that we do better to avoid them altogether. Some people call themselves atheists for no other reason than that they are sick to the teeth of the denominational faith industry and of the non-denominational and anti-denominational cult manufacturing that leaves next to no room for decency, for ordinary respectful behaviour and good common sense. Even decency and common sense have been hijacked by liberalist theologians and rationalist evangelists. It's as if one final competition were on for the last few human souls that are left. Do we not feel secure until we have a label hanging around our necks? Journalist - Christian - Capitalist - Anthroposophist - Socialist - Housewife - God-seeker - Workingman - Feminist: these are labels and we hide behind them or beat one another over the head with them. When you go to the toilet, bolt the door, appreciate the peace and quiet and confer with your maker. Jesus lives in your heart, you don't need to be forever advertising his image. The messiah is here and now, god is merciful love and your father, there, basta. Now don't keep repeating that; the creative spirit does not take kindly to being stretched on the rack.

You are telling me, in other words, that when I teach religion I should be demonstrating god rather than talking about God. And I can make a special effort, especially since I intend to relate much more directly to the human nature and to the world circumstances of my pupils than if I were teaching them how to add and subtract, or if I were introducing them to some poetry.

*

An important issue is something that can be called the religious mood. Here we have to be extremely careful, because so much that has to do with mood, and with moods, is sentimentalized and emotionalized and artificialized. I am thinking of drugs, especially, and of the mass media.

If we think of religion as the mending and healing of the tear between outside world and inside self, then mood is religion insofar as it goes on right now and inasmuch as I am doing it right now. Mood is itself the fact that the two are being made one and that they're becoming one. Probably we only know of moods, not of mood. We are in a good mood or in a bad mood. But when we are in a mood, we have already become exiles from the religious process. So in that sense a religious mood, or the religious mood, is really something that has either been artificially stimulated, such as through LSD or repetitious prayings, or else it has come about through self-indulgence, in self-pity, misery and such like. These are unfortunate substitutes for the real thing. A mood is something that can be identified; we can, so to speak, put our finger on it, and certainly we should not foster moods, or seek them out or produce them, neither in ourselves nor in others. Religion as mood can not be identified. We can say that it is, but not what or where it is. The mystery of religion as mood has to be taken into account by the teacher of religion, and he must guard carefully against moods of any sort. When a mood is upon him he must simply deny it and say: get behind me.

The teacher of religion is very much aware of this mystery when he takes up with his pupils the aspects of their everyday world experience and the various strains of their everyday inward experience. Mysteriously he holds these two spheres - or hemispheres - together in himself. Take note now how this can be talked about and how it can not be talked about. The mood of the teacher is not religious but religion. He cannot be in this mood and he cannot have it. We might, at times, suppose we are 'in God' but we are only in a religious mood. We might suppose we have religion, but once again all we have is such a religious mood. Eastern sages and western mystics have referred to religion-as-mood, as 'that which is and is not', as 'an insensible stirring of the heart'. It is 'the sound of one hand clapping', or 'the possession of our soul in patience'. The last one makes the most sense to me because it indicates the doing of religion gracefully and with ease.

A teacher of religion must know religion as mood while he teaches. If his being is not stayed and his mind is not stable in this mystery, how can he gather in, for his pupils, their diverse and divergent experiences? If he allows himself to get into a mood, good or bad, and if he cannot get past such moods, he will actually mislead his pupils. If he tries to stimulate or produce moods of one sort or another, such as a religious mood, he will actually teach children how to falsify religion. He himself must know the mystery of mood, and of course he realizes that not a child is born that does not bring with it into the world a capacity for religion, an aptitude for religion as mood and a taste for this mystery. By harbouring this mystery in himself – the mystery which one philosopher formulated as: "man is to man a god," – a teacher of religion simply reminds his pupils of their inheritance. Let's face it, he teaches them religion because they have already lost track of some of it and because he wishes to help them invest it as universal experience.

But he also keeps in mind – and in fact the harbouring of this mood-mystery in himself won't allow him to forget – that children have something like dream-wisdom which he in his adult wide-awake cleverness has perhaps forfeited. The mood of religion testifies to the bond of truth that links us all, if we but knew it and acted accordingly. Teachers of religion relate to their pupils by way of this intimate bond and they rely on it immediately. As they rely on it to do its work, it turns into something we call, with right, piety.

True piety is demonstrated by the teacher of religion as he relies on the mysterious mood of religion. This piety lets young human beings know that at the centre of the universe a warm heart beats. Such knowledge strengthens immensely. It is not only a comfort, but an encouragement and food for real ambition towards excellence. Piety is the adult's mature form of the child's inborn security. The pious adult shows that he has something on which he can essentially depend and rely. Sometimes we suppose that moral principles make for a reliable and dependable adult, for someone who holds what he promises and practices what he preaches, but piety is greater than moral principles, and where piety turns into mere piousness because no religion is done, actually done, in spirit, soul and flesh, moral principles become coercive and destructive. The force of a moral principle is a deadly weapon that cripples even the one who wields it.

A teacher of religion will never attempt to bring about a religious mood, not in himself and not in his pupils. Such an effort is disastrous. It's dishonest and false, and the very best pupil will be the one who says: No! Not under any circumstances! - And then he will be called the worst, which is almost a criminal injustice. People are forever rushing to produce such a religious mood, and we hanker for it because it lets us suppose we are good. No, religion as mood is like a sign that religion is at work, and yet its absence does not imply that religion is not at work. In terms of religion we can reach so high and so far, so deep and so near, in safety, soundness and health, that the truth and the light in person touches us of its own free will. Religion as mood is not at our command and it makes no sense to strive for it, but until we come into the enjoyment of it and into the patient possession of it we know and can take for granted that all our efforts at religion are well worthwhile.

A teacher of religion is, above all else, secure in himself in his relation to his - not fellow man, but fellow men, women and children. He holds no grudges, forgives readily, is slow to anger but capable of anger. He typecasts no one, condemns no one and is never critical. Unless of course it happens to him that he does these things, and then he chooses contrition. He prefers peace, but is capable of compromise. And - not to be underesti-

mated - he is a teacher of religion while he teaches religion, not before or afterwards. Let him beware of jargon
and labels. The rudiments of his craft are contained in his
heart, of his art in his spirit.

* * *

36. Will-power and Art

We have to be careful, because we think force is an
instrument. Really we try to make force do where a much
more lenient approach, coupled with insight, would render results more surprising. The lack of will-power
frightens us, because the matter in hand, the raw materials, refuse to turn into the product. And we know of the
product. We have it in mind. We picture and predict it.
We even perhaps harbour an idea of it. Then our art goes
awry. We suffer a disappointment. The fruits of our la-
bours collapse.

The point is, we tried to manoeuvre them into some
likely representation. They resented this. We cajoled.
They balked. We threatened. Then they called our bluff.
Because what, after all, can we do, when we threaten to
destroy the thing we want to build? Who stands to lose,
except ourselves?

So one thing remains: to throw in the towel. If it
won't allow us to whip it into shape, the thing isn't worthy of our attention. We should never have condescended
in the first place.

Education as an art has the mature human being as its
product. What we call our will, and what we mean by
will-power, this has to be looked at carefully if we mean
to teach in this way, where a pupil seems to say to us:
"Make me behave in the way you prefer," and then, when

233

we give it a go, the relationship breaks down and our intentions fly back at us. Pupils have a way of looking at us then as if we must be crazy, to expect such a thing of them as our will-power dictates, while we demand justice, which we blatantly define as compliance with our will.

Consider for a moment the nature of will as appetite. The thing we imagine as worthy of attainment - for this we have an appetite. Our nature desires to unite with the thing we attain. Love can play into this. I would love a T-bone steak! I would love a mature pupil! The stupid, ill-behaved pupil stands between us and our goal, which is a union of us with the mature pupil. We get into the bad habit of pursuing along a straight line the object of our desire - of our love - of our will.

Now the one thing we leave out of consideration entirely, when we behave like this, is what the product of our art itself desires to become. As soon as we allow for that, we notice that we mean a being, that lives, and not a thing, that does not live. Anything we do in the way of an art, education for example, implies a contemplation of being as live. What should we call it, in comparison, when we limit ourselves to the shaping of things that are dead? But that's just it, we don't in fact limit ourselves. No, it comes over us, especially when we get into a rage out of sheer impatience. Suddenly we forget that these are beings and we behave as though they were things, and as though they existed for our sake. No, worse, as though they existed for our gratification.

We begin with the intention to teach a being artfully and find ourselves suddenly punishing a thing that re-

fuses to gratify our self. We even see it happening, sometimes, and yet are powerless to stop it, to turn the process
round, so that we should cease from destruction and return to art. It sickens us, this powerlessness. It wears us
out and grinds us down.

Our will, it seems, has its own agenda and enrols us in
its plans. How the devil does that happen? Patient loving
kindness is swept aside and bowled over by strident self-
assertion. The being we wish to influence eludes our
grasp, escapes from us - asserts its own will, perhaps, -
while we are left behind guilty and ashamed. Many a good
teacher has wept hot tears of frustration over yet again just
such an experience. Many an obliging pupil has stepped
back perplexed, has stepped out of the relationship inwardly, to remain only for form's sake, because the risks
were too great.

And what are the risks, from the point of view of the
perplexed pupil? There is the risk of damage to the spirit,
of harm to the soul. But let's keep this in perspective.
The pupil has some idea of his spirit, he has a notion of
his soul, and these, the idea and the notion, are in fact
what is at risk, not the actual soul or spirit of the human
being in the teacher-pupil relationship.

And of course there is no reason under the sun why
this idea and this notion should be damaged or harmed.
All the same, it happens, and frequently. All one can say
is: what a pity! Once my soul is my own it cannot be
harmed and once my spirit is my own it cannot be damaged. They are truly mine when they function maturely.
But the pupil still aims at maturity. Therefore his idea of
his spirit may be damaged and his notion of his soul may

be harmed. The mature teacher has it as his goal that the pupil should come into the mature possession of his spirit and soul. He also sees, and recognizes, and perhaps acknowledges, the pupil's ideas and notions of spirit and soul.

Can we trace the profile of the conflict? Do we sense the animosity that can crop up, of the teacher's will against the pupil's ideas and notions? Do we not feel how important it must always be for the teacher not to confront these ideas and notions but instead to address the productive relationship - in terms of his own mature spirit and soul, which cannot be damaged or harmed, as the teacher well knows?

Of course the teacher must try his best not to do the damage or harm we have described. But accidents will happen. Then let him call to mind that he has not done something irreversible. He has merely added to the mortification of the pupil, from which he should have been taking away. What is required then is simply the appropriate apology. This apology consists a marked demonstration by the teacher that he can in fact keep his poor ego under and that he is able to sustain a relationship in spite of temptations to become overbearing and to undermine. Not only teachers, every parental adult knows this temptation and soon learns how relationships are strengthened every time such ego confrontation is simply avoided - mercifully.

Mercy is the single successful corrective where the self looks for ways to insist on its right. The problem is complicated where an adult is to educate children, or to bring them up. For the adult feels called upon to provoke or to repress the child and he supposes that justice demands this. And against an immature adult a child has no defence.

But mercy puts all things to right. The pupil's notions and ideas of soul and spirit do not need to be sacrificed any more in the interest of artificial goals and egotistical ambitions, because the teacher himself is more mindful of common humanity than of ideas and notions. He learns to confront in himself every merciless impulse so that it cannot run wild. Much that parades as order, as discipline and justice, and especially as virtuous sacrifice, is nothing but mercilessness in fact. To be merciless means to convict someone of a fault of which he is not, and perhaps even cannot be, aware. Now we should not even convict someone of a fault he knows, because there we should forgive. But to convict someone of a fault he does not know means adding insult to injury. What we need to confirm in ourselves is the knowledge that we have neither the wisdom nor the right to convict one another; such conviction must come from quite another department. Where we leave it to the good spirit to convict, we may harvest fruitful growth, but where we insist on doing it ourselves we end up condemned in ourselves.

Education as art is especially prone to wilful conviction because so many opportunities exist for mercy. Let those who incline to acts of wilfulness take on board the glad news that by sheer force of will we may repress our potential mercilessness and come up with the fine wine of mercy. If you have a forceful will and are prone to accidents, no need to court humiliation. Simply learn to work the winepress of mercy.

* * * * *

www.ingramcontent.com/pod-product-compliance
Lightning Source LLC
Chambersburg PA
CBHW060454290526
45791CB00001B/107